CULTURE CARE

Reconnecting with Beauty for our Common Life

Makoto Fujimura

Published and Produced by the Fujimura Institute
and International Arts Movement
38 West 39th Street, 3rd floor
New York, NY 10018
212-944-0944

www.fujimurainstitute.org
www.internationalartsmovement.org

Frontispiece: *Ki-Seki*
© 2014 Makoto Fujimura
Mineral Pigments, Sumi ink, silver, and gold on Kumohada paper
60.25 x 45.25 x 1.25 in
Private Collection

Edited by Peter Edman

Designed by Lindsay Kolk

Printed in the USA by Deschamps Printing, Salem, MA

ISBN 978-1-4951-3163-9

Dedicated to those who sowed seeds of generativity into my life, starting with Judy and my parents.

I would like to thank Ann Smith for her care in the initial editing process, Peter Edman for his extensive editorial contributions, Lindsay Kolk for her beautiful design, Amy Jones and Mark Rodgers of Wedgwood Circle for their encouragement to publish the introductory booklet for Culture Care called "On Becoming Generative," the Deschamps printing team for printing the award-winning booklet, as well as the many people who supported the Kickstarter campaign making the publication of this book possible. I also gratefully acknowledge the board and staff of International Arts Movement, past and present, for their modeling Culture Care values even before we named them, particularly Chris and Barbara Giammona for their support of the creation of this book. Annie Dwyer has been an invaluable executive assistant, especially in helping me carve out the time needed to complete this work.

I am also grateful for my wife and my children who are constant reminders of beauty to me.

Contents

Preface

This is a book for artists, but artists come in many forms. Anyone with a calling to create—from visual artists, musicians, writers, and actors, to entrepreneurs, pastors, and business professionals—will resonate with its message. This book is for anyone who feels the cultural divide, especially those with a desire or an artistic gift to reach across boundaries with understanding, reconciliation, and healing. It is a book for anyone with a passion for the arts, for supporters of the arts, and for "creative catalysts" who understand how much the culture we all share affects human thriving today and shapes the generations to come.

Culture Care, though a thesis I have developed, is a movement already afoot in culture in various circles. In one sense, this book is not new or unique; International Arts Movement and the Fujimura Institute are part of a whole ecosystem of a greater movement. But having acknowledged that, this is a book that addresses head-on a terrible rift in our society: our culture is broken and needs care to be restored to wholeness. Like the "Creation Care" movement that looks after the environment, and the "Soul Care" concepts provided by practitioners in mental health and spiritual growth, this book on Culture Care lays out a necessary conceptual framework and the beginnings of practical responses to repair that rift. This is a book meant to inspire individuals and to inform the wider movement in providing such care.

Since the publication of the small booklet called "On Becoming Generative: An Introduction to Culture Care" (included with minor adaptations here) much has already happened in public conversations about culture. Recently, I was with Dr. James Davison Hunter at the University of Virginia's Institute for Advanced Studies in Culture, a sociologist widely known for his groundbreaking work on the American culture wars. He affirmed this journey toward Culture Care, noting that poetry (and the arts in general) and generative thinking are critical for our society to begin a shift away from our corrosive culture battles.

While I base my thinking and applications from a Christian perspective and often work with people within Christian communities, this thesis is not limited to Christians. The principles of Culture Care can be embraced universally. They depend only on developing skills in listening to the wider culture, and thereby becoming a loving servant toward culture rather than treating it as territory to be won.

Some people may find what I term a Christian perspective debatable, nebulous, meaningless, or even offensive, but I dare to suggest that this book may be helpful even for such people. As I explain in the book, my thesis, flowing out of my pilgrimage with Jesus of Nazareth, has led me into a wider journey, discovering my role as a "border-stalker," moving in and out of arts institutions, churches, and other organizations. I write this from the margins of all these diverse forms of infrastructure, and hoping to speak into the hearts of all those who desire to seek the truth and fill the world again with beauty.

Two words of thanks: The initial spark that led to the coinage of the term "Culture Care" came from my friend and executive editor, Caleb Seeling. It was in a car, on a winding road to the Aspen Institute, that he suggested I consider writing this book. Thanks also to Mark Rodgers and Amy Jones of the Wedgwood Circle for initiating the printing of the first Culture Care booklet, which has garnered so much attention.

On Becoming Generative

Bringing beauty into our lives

As a newlywed couple, my wife and I began our journey with very little. After Judy and I got married in the summer of 1983, after college, we moved to Connecticut for Judy to pursue her master's degree in marriage counseling. I taught at a special education school and painted at home. We had a tight budget and often had to ration our food (lots of tuna cans!) just to get through the week.

One evening, I am sitting alone, waiting for Judy to come home to our small apartment, worried about how we are going to afford the rent, to pay for necessities over the weekend. Our refrigerator is empty and I have no cash left.

Then Judy walks in, and she has brought home a bouquet of flowers. I get really upset.

"How could you think of buying flowers if we can't even eat!" I remember saying, frustrated.

Judy's reply has been etched in my heart for over thirty years now. *"We need to feed our souls, too."*

The irony is that I am an artist. I am the one, supposedly, feeding people's souls. But in worrying for tomorrow, in the stoic responsibility I feel to make ends meet, to survive, I fail to be the artist. Judy is the artist: she brings home a bouquet.

I do not remember what we ended up eating that day, or that month (probably tuna fish).

But I do remember that particular bouquet of flowers. I painted them.

"We *need* to feed our souls, too." Those words still resonate with me today.

Is Judy still right? Do we, as human beings, need more than food and shelter? Do we need beauty in our lives? Given our limited resources, how do we cultivate and care for our souls? And how do these questions apply to the larger culture?

My life as an artist, and as a founder of International Arts Movement, has been in pursuit of questions like these—not just internally or for my own sake but with a growing global network of people. What began as an admission of my own failure to be an artist has now given birth to many principles that govern my life as an artist, father, husband, and leader. I call them "generative principles." What started out as Judy's care for our own souls has blossomed into an effort to extend that care into our home and our churches, and into a vision for culture at large. What I call Culture Care is a generative approach to culture that brings bouquets of flowers into a culture bereft of beauty.

An artist's journey toward generativity

I have found that what I am asked to do often seems impossible. How can I make a living as an artist? How can I support my family as an artist? How can I support a family and a growing movement as an artist? These challenges seem to expand with every opportunity, but in my mind they come back to the same generative principles.

This essay launches a series of essays and conversations on Culture Care, to which I invite the contributions of artists, curators, critics, patrons, and other lovers of the arts and participants in culture. To help frame the conversation for different types of thinkers, I begin by briefly considering "three G's" sparked by Judy's act that have come to characterize my approach to generative thinking:

1. *genesis moments,*
2. *generosity, and*
3. *generational thinking.*

In the next section, I will draw these elements together with more formal definitions of the terms "generative" and "culture care" to help frame and catalyze an ongoing conversation.

Bringing home a bouquet of flowers created a *genesis moment* for me. Judy's small act fed my soul. It renewed my conviction as an artist. It gave me new perspective. It challenged me to deliberately focus on endeavors in which I could truly be an artist of the soul. That moment engendered many more genesis moments in the years that followed, contributing to decisions small and large that have redefined my life and provided inspiration for myself, my family, and my communities.

Genesis moments like this often include elements of the great story told in the beginning of the biblical book of Genesis: creativity, growth—and failure. Two of these are common in discussions about arts and culture. God creates and calls his creatures to fruitfulness. Adam exercises his own creativity in naming what has been created. But the story also runs into failure and finitude.

Generative thinking often starts out with a failure, like my failure to think and act as an artist. I have discovered that something is awakened through failure, tragedy, and disappointment. It is a place of learning and potential creativity. In such moments, you can get lost in despair or denial, or you can recognize the failure and run toward the hope of something new.

The genesis moment is to assume every moment is fresh. Creativity applied in a moment of weakness and vulnerability can turn failure into enduring conversation, opening new vistas of inspiration and incarnation. To remember what Judy did, to speak of it with others, to value her care—all this is generative, as her act can be honored and become a touchpoint for others, leading to the birth of ideas and actions, artifacts and relationships that would not otherwise have been.

The bouquet was also an emblem of *generosity*. Judy's generous heart—more generous than mine at that moment—valued beauty over the day-to-day worries that had so nearly narrowed my focus. Generative thinking is fueled by generosity because it so often must work against a mindset that has survival and utility in the foreground. In a culture like that, generosity has an unexpectedness that can set the context for the renewal of our hearts. An encounter with generosity can remind us that life always overflows our attempts to reduce it to a commodity or a transaction—because it is a gift. Life and beauty are gratuitous in the best senses of that word.

Judy's generosity with the bouquet is only one of many instances of generosity in my life. I was able to become an artist partly because of my parents' generosity and encouragement. Both my father and my mother encouraged to me when I desired to pursue the arts. That, for an Asian family, was extremely unusual. Music, painting, writing, and creating have always been part of my life. I took them for granted, and thought that everyone's homes were a nurturing environment for creativity. Then I went to middle school and discovered I was an anomaly! It was then that I started to realize I somehow had to defend my time for creativity in a culture that does not nurture creative growth.

Artists have a deep capacity to develop and share generosity and empathy, to point toward abundance and connections. We learn generosity as we try to communicate with a new audience, or help people express what they cannot otherwise articulate, or say something meaningful into the void. Even an artist who journeys alone, like the poet Emily Dickinson, can develop a sense of communicating or communing with someone—the reader, nature, God—and so strengthen critical generative capacities to bring beauty into the world. An encounter with the arts can lead to generative thinking as generosity supplants our *quid pro quo* expectations. (In the sciences, too, discovery is linked to the generosity of information shared among its practitioners.) The effects begin with gratitude and lead to places we cannot predict.

As I reflect on Judy's simple act and on my life in the arts, I am more and more convinced that anything truly generative is not isolated. Generative values are given to us as a gift by our parents and predecessors. They grow in conversation with the past and in our intention to speak and create so as to cultivate the values of multiple future generations. Generative thinking requires *generational thinking*.

Culture formation is generational, not birthed in a night. Generative thinking can inspire us to work within a vision for culture that is expressed in centuries and millennia rather than quarters, seasons, or fashions. People in the arts work in conversation with artists of the past as they are preparing the future, attempting work with enduring qualities that might in turn speak to new generations.

I have seen gratuitous acts modeled by Judy's parents and family. I have failed at times to appreciate my own parents' generosity—but at least have had the receptivity to repent! My father's generosity in particular has led to so many blessings in the world that he did not expect or even realize—all flowing from his love for art and music. Such acts from our parents are now reflected in unexpected ways not least in the lives of our creative children, all of whom deeply value beauty and model generosity.

Even the term "generative" is a gift to me. My father, Osamu Fujimura, is a pioneer of acoustics research. I was born in Boston because he was doing post-doctoral research at MIT with Noam Chomsky. Recently, I invited him to attend an International Arts Movement (IAM) conference. As we walked together to the TriBeCa Performance Center where I was about to give a keynote, he asked me what I was to speak on. I told him the speech would be "On

Generative Culture." My father responded, "Interesting ... the word 'generative' ... that was my thesis topic."

I knew that. I had even read the thesis. But for some reason I had sidelined this influence and forgotten to link my theme to his lifetime of work! He was instrumental in bringing Chomsky's Generative Grammar Theory to Japan. I was grateful for the rediscovery and was able to present my version of generative thinking with a proper attribution of his influence.

Our lives are directed or constrained by paths paved by the generations before us. Sometimes we can trace them, as with my father. Often they shape us unawares. What is true of legacies from our parents is true also for our communities and racial and national histories. Cultures are not created overnight. We are affected by layers of experiences, personalities, and works of previous generations. Cultural histories affect us far beyond what we are able to recognize—or sometimes admit.

Generative principles flow out of generational blessing toward creativity. But the positive examples of my wife and parents are all too rare. Many people look back on what can seem to be generational curses rather than blessings. I created IAM—and continue to advocate for the arts—from a conviction that all people need a place of nurture toward their creative growth. Acts of generosity can inspire genesis moments even from generational failures.

This book is the first in a series on Culture Care that will expand on these and other generative principles and apply them to several cases. It is my hope to engender conversations and so gather a community of people committed to generative living. This, it should be emphasized, is not an end in itself but a contribution to the greater good. Generative paths will birth resourcefulness, patience, and general creativity in all of life. They lead to cultural—and human—thriving.

Culture Care
Defined

Culture Care is to provide care for our culture's "soul," to bring
to our cultural home our bouquet of flowers, so that reminders of
beauty—both ephemeral and enduring—are present in even the
harshest environments where survival is at stake. We may need
to learn to cultivate these reminders of beauty in the same way
flowers are cared for and raised. Culture Care restores beauty as a
seed of invigoration into the ecosystem of culture. Such soul care
is generative: a well-nurtured culture becomes an environment in
which people and creativity thrive.

At this point it will be helpful to gather the threads to find a working
definition of our terms. At the most basic level, we call something
"generative" if it is fruitful, originating new life or producing
offspring (as with plants and animals) or producing new parts (as
with stem cells). When we are generative, we draw on creativity to
bring into being something fresh and life-giving.

We can also approach generativity by looking at its shadow,
"degenerate," the loss of good or desirable qualities (a term also
frequently used of generations). What is generative is the opposite
of degrading or limiting. It is constructive, expansive, affirming,
growing beyond a mindset of scarcity.

One of Chomsky's early definitions of "generative grammar" refers to
the set of rules that can be used to create or generate all grammatical
sentences in a language. He was looking in human languages, as
did my father in his work in acoustics, for a universal generative
principle, an explanation of our ability to generate seemingly
infinite phrases by switching out elements from a finite vocabulary
and grammatical framework. Building on this, we might say that

a generative approach will identify and model the "grammar" or conditions that best contribute to a good life and a thriving culture.

Discovering and naming this grammar, identifying and then living truly generative principles, is a process that depends deeply on generosity. This is because it requires us to open ourselves to deep questions (and to their answers), which is impossible when survival seems to depend on competing for scarce resources. But when we acknowledge the gratuitous nature of life—not least the world's inordinately diverse beauty—gratitude galvanizes us to ask and welcome questions that reach beyond our own context and experience. Artists at their best help us with such questions by presenting an expansive vision of life that reveals beauty in ever-wider zones.

Such a vision is by its nature a challenge to dictators and totalitarian regimes—a threat to those whose power depends on holding humanity at the level of survival or, worse, on eliminating diverse elements from societies. Artists and other generative people can sense dehumanizing trends quickly, and this is why they are often targeted by autocrats. But artists, ultimately, can reveal new facets of human flourishing even in the midst of tragedy or horror, pointing toward hope and meaning.

Another key generative principle emerges as we begin to escape the cramped thinking of a culture of scarcity: stewardship. Beyond mere survival, beyond job function, bureaucratic specialization, or social roles, is a wide scope of human concern and responsibility. We are all given gifts for which we all must care. Just as we are learning the importance of taking care of our environment to leave the earth healthy for future generations, so we must all care for culture so future generations can thrive.

Implied in the above themes is a measure by which to assess principles that claim to be generative: Thinking and living that are truly generative make possible works and movements that make our culture more humane and welcoming and that inspire us to be more fully human. We can be comfortable, even confident, in affirming a cultural contribution as generative if, over time, it recognizes, produces, or catalyzes more beauty, goodness, and flourishing.

What emerges from generative moments is something new, transformed from its source, something that is both free and responsible to make its own ongoing creative contribution. I have on my farm a magnificent old pear tree. This tree has grown from a small seed. First, the seed died. It found welcoming soil and morphed into a tiny shoot. In time, with nurture, it came to full growth, a thing of beauty at many levels, all on a scale out of proportion to the original seed, and full of generative potential in its turn. The tree provides shade and shelter, flowers and fruit. It might provide wood for warmth or walls or works of art. It might contribute to a landscape or resist erosion. It might inspire poems or plays, paintings or photographs (such as the *Ki-Seki* painting at front of the book). It might spark a scientific discovery, host children at play, or lead a man or woman to reflect on the nature of life.

We can say that Culture Care is applied generative thinking. Culture Care ultimately results in a generative cultural environment: open to questions of meaning, reaching beyond mere survival, inspiring people to meaningful action, and leading toward wholeness and harmony. It produces thriving cross-generational community.

Interlude: When beauty was taboo

By intentionally using the word "beauty," I am swimming upstream. When I began to exhibit in New York City in the mid-nineties, "beauty" was a taboo, not to be spoken of in public. It signified cultural hegemony, imperialist power, the corruption of the past, or the cosmetic sheen of superficial contemporary culture. The art world still resists this word.

The first time I spoke at Dillon Gallery in SoHo, I quoted the sacred text of Isaiah 61:2–3:

> *... to comfort all who mourn,*
> *and provide for those who grieve in Zion—*

> *to bestow on them a crown of beauty*
> *instead of ashes,*
> *the oil of joy*
> *instead of mourning,*
> *and a garment of praise*
> *instead of a spirit of despair.*

At times in my own journey, even long after Judy's reminder of a bouquet of flowers, I have struggled to incorporate beauty into my life. As a National Scholar graduate student in Japan, studying the art of Nihonga, I found myself using such extravagantly beautiful materials as gold, silver, malachite, azurite, and exquisite paper and silk. I wrestled with beauty revealed in front of me, created with my own hands. I did not then have a conceptual framework to incorporate beauty as a valid premise of contemporary art. At that first artist's talk at Dillon Gallery, I spoke of this struggle, and how, on finding the central reality of Jesus Christ, I was for the first time able to find in Christ himself an integrating premise behind beauty.

For Christ also began his ministry with a reading from Isaiah 61.

> *The Spirit of the Lord is on me,*
> *because he has anointed me*
> *to proclaim good news to the poor.*

> *He has sent me to proclaim freedom for the prisoners*
> *and recovery of sight for the blind,*
> *to set the oppressed free … (Luke 4:18)*

Then he shocked those in the audience by claiming that "Today this Scripture has been fulfilled in your hearing." Jesus of Nazareth claimed to be the one who can provide for us a "crown of beauty instead of ashes." He claimed to be the source of this beauty.

In mentioning beauty—let alone Christ—in a room filled with people of the art world, I knew that I was transgressing against what was culturally acceptable for them. But as his follower, I needed to acknowledge Christ's claims, to hold them up in this public sphere as something we can test. I wanted to begin to reclaim beauty, and to frame it for our time as a gift given to us by the Creator. I wanted to help recover a view of beauty as a gift that we discover, receive, and steward.

The next day, a critic who was in the audience called and surprised me by saying: "I have never heard anybody quote Isaiah in the art world and mean it with conviction. I was moved by what you had to say." Thus began a journey to create and present beauty in the harsh and cynical environment of the New York art world.

Working assumptions

The framework of Culture Care rests on a number of foundational assumptions. Many resemble what one might expect when applying the principles of environmental stewardship (known in some circles as creation care) to cultural stewardship. I am assuming that efforts to restore the cultural environment are good and noble, and that our efforts will benefit the next generation. I am assuming that an attempt to speak with people through conversations and questions that are outside the current cultural and ideological divide is healthy and will ultimately help culture thrive.

As a Christian, I find the source and goal of beauty, of generative thinking, and of responsible action in the biblical understanding of what our lives are for. We find our creative identity in God. Genesis moments can be assumed simply because God is the great Artist, and we are God's artists, called to steward the creation entrusted to our care. The good news of the Bible is that in Christ we are journeying toward ultimate wholeness, integration, and well-being. We are becoming more fully what we were made to be, to the benefit of all creation.

But Culture Care and generative principles are not concepts only for Christian believers or churches or religious conversations.

Culture Care is everyone's business. Everyone can—and I gratefully acknowledge that many people from all sorts of backgrounds do—

contribute to the common good. These conversations are open to all people of good will. To make culture inhabitable, to make it a place of nurture for creativity, we must all choose to give away beauty gratuitously.

"Gratuitous" can be a negative word, as in "gratuitous violence," but here I am using it to speak of intentionality, and even forcefulness, which, as we will see in later chapters, is necessary in our deeply fragmented culture. I will also be looking at how the reality of beauty can help integrate such fragmentation.

Black River,
Cracked Lands

People in Western cultures often think of themselves first as individuals, but the human being may be better understood as a focal point of embedded relationships. Sometimes we are more aware of our dependence and sometimes we are more aware of our contributions, but we exist in community—in families, in places. In churches and work groups. In economies and ecologies. What is more, our multifaceted interactions with our physical and cultural environment directly affect our bodies, our minds, our spirits, and ultimately our souls.

We can talk about all these elements separately, but we cannot actually isolate our reactions (much as we might like to). Any experience that affects our relationships affects our minds, which affect our bodies, and so on, back and forth. If we are to thrive, we can do so only as part of a wider interrelated ecosystem. Thriving ecosystems are known for abundance and diversity, hospitable even to those who want to dwell as outliers and remain in the margins.

Judy reminded us that our souls need food as well as our bodies. We will discuss how beauty feeds the soul in a later chapter, but first we should address the related question of the consequences when the soul is starved. What happens to communities when our souls are fed from the produce of a polluted ecosystem? This is the situation in which we live today. We need to be aware of the greater cultural reality that is causing this imbalance so that we can find the best path toward Culture Care.

An industrial map in the mid-twentieth century colored New York's Hudson River black. The mapmakers considered a black river a good thing—full of industry! The more factory outputs, the more progress.

When that map was made, "nature" was widely seen as a resource to be exploited. Few people considered the consequences of careless disposal of industrial waste. The culture has shifted dramatically over the last fifty years. When I share this story today, most people shudder and ask how anyone could think of a polluted river as good.

But today we are doing the same thing with the river of culture. Think of the arts and other cultural enterprises as rivers that water the soil of culture. We are painting this cultural river black—full of industry, dominated by commercial interests, careless of toxic byproducts—and there are still cultural mapmakers who claim that this is a good thing. The pollution makes it difficult to for us to breathe, difficult for artists to create, difficult for any of us to see beauty through the murk.

It is widely recognized that our culture today is not life-giving. There is little room at the margins to make artistic endeavors sustainable. The wider ecosystem of art and culture has been decimated, leaving only homogeneous pockets of survivors, those fit enough to survive in a poisoned environment. In culture as in nature, a lack of diversity is a first sign of a distressed ecosystem.

Many of the streams that feed the river of culture are polluted, and the soil this river should be watering is thus parched and fragmented. Most of these we know, but let me briefly touch on some of the fault lines in the cultural soil (starving the soul) as well as some of the sources of the poisons in the water (polluting the soul).

Starving the cultural soul

One of the most powerful sources of cultural fragmentation has grown out of the great successes of the industrial revolution. Its vision, standards, and methods soon proliferated beyond the factory and the economic realm and were embraced in sectors from education to government and even church. The result was reductionism. Modern people began to equate progress with efficiency. Despite valiant and ongoing resistance from many quarters—including industry—success for a large part of our culture is now judged by efficient production and mass consumption. We often value repetitive, machine-like performance as critical to "bottom line" success. In the seductive industrialist mentality, "people" become "workers" or "human resources," who are first seen as interchangeable cogs, then treated as machines—and are now often replaced by machines.

A related cultural fault line is hyperspecialization, where a person or firm focuses on increasingly narrow segments of a production process, a discipline, an artistic genre, or a market. One result is an increasing prominence in our culture of the "expert." The expert knows one part, not the whole, and often not even the wider field in which they work. They consciously reduce their scope of concern to go deeper in their discipline. But increased clarity on a narrow point usually comes at the price of blindness to context and to one's working assumptions. It often brings isolation from—and sometimes alienation from or hostility to—those with differing expertise.

Today's expert usually shies away from questions of meaning and connection and responsibility—referring such issues to those who "specialize" in meaning. This is, of course, fundamentally unsatisfying for human beings and contributes to our cultural unease. It also has troubling consequences within a discipline. My father's career offers an example of this.[1]

My father spent years at Tokyo University after his research with Chomsky, and later joined the famed Bell Laboratories pure-research complex in Murray Hill, New Jersey. It was at Bell Labs in the early 1970s that he began to notice fundamental deficiencies in acoustics research. In the 1980s, in his early fifties, my father began to send a series of notes to his colleagues questioning basic tenets of their field. He found many of their approaches flawed because they were based on reductionist assumptions. They did not fit the data and were thus inadequate and unable to reach their stated goals.

1 I write about this episode in the essay "Refractions #24," which can be found at my website makotofujimura.com.

In my simplified understanding, the early research assumed that
you could generate enough data to rebuild speech by segmenting
speech patterns. It seems a bit like dissecting a frog and stitching it
back together, only to expect it to jump again—a typical modernist
approach. They expected to be able to simulate natural-sounding
human speech within a decade and they predicted the rise of
technologies like Apple's Siri and Google's voice navigation. But my
father was right. Even the best such technologies thirty years later
sound choppy and machine-like.

Even dealing with a community of scientists—who are supposed to
be known for their mental flexibility—it took years before my father
could present his new ideas to the linguistics/phonetics community.
Many tenured professors, I am sure, found his claims threatening
to their assumptions. My father had never, prior to this time, had
problems finding support for his research, but now he found himself
fighting the research establishment that he had himself helped to
build. After many futile attempts to secure funding, my brother, a
successful Silicon Valley entrepreneur, stepped in to fund a post for a
graduate student to help my father compile enough data to begin
his research.

That today's computer voices sound as good as they do is in part
the result of my father's work. After the breakup of AT&T in the
eighties, he spent many years at Ohio State trying to introduce a new
path called C/D (Converter/Distributor) theory. This theory is not
so much concerned with segmenting language as on recognizing
patterns of vocal stress and intonation. He calls this approach
prosodic, as it better accounts for the natural complexity of speech
and language.

Most of us recognize the shortcomings of reductionism at a deep
level: we know that we are more than what we produce, that
efficiency is not the point of education, of religion, of art, of play, or
of many other aspects of human culture. Most people are dissatisfied
with the reductionist viewpoint, yet not enough of us have or can

articulate viable alternatives because it has taken over not only how people define success, but also what we value in society. Many in our culture no longer value a bouquet of flowers because beauty contributes neither to the machinery of production nor to an advantage in the latest cultural battle—and because the pressure for continued consumption warps our capacity to appreciate and enjoy.

It is not the desire to survive or to provide for a family that is problematic. Cultural fragmentation comes rather when we fall into the trap of treating survival as the bottom line and thus neglect the holistic approaches that demand personal growth and point our civilization toward a greater vision. Fragmentation comes when we forget the importance of beauty for our lives and the necessity—for both individual and social flourishing—of sharing the experience of beauty in community.

In the face of reductionism, we must recall that human beings are not "human doings," as one of my mentors[2] says. We are more than animals following our instincts to compete and survive. Human culture encompasses more than loyalty to a den, herd, or pack. Our concern as individuals and families should thus be to raise, educate, and form whole persons—to cultivate connected citizens who can co-create thriving communities, cities, and nations.

Polluting the cultural soul

I see the fragmentation and reductionism operating in culture today as releasing two main pollutants into the river of culture. They are what I call *over-commodification of art* and *utilitarian pragmatism*. Today, instead of regarding art as a visionary gift to society, we see it as a means for commercial gain. Those artists who aspire to anything other than market success are often caught up in the culture wars, their works put to use as ideological tools—or weapons—in those divisive struggles. These pollutants are choking the creatures that should be swimming and contributing to the diversity of expression. Reductionism is no stranger to the arts. What my father

---

2   Thank you, Nigel Goodwin, for the "Nigelisms" that continue to encourage us. He often finishes the phrase: "and we are human becomings."

experienced as a scientist in battling against reductionism, artists were experiencing very early in the twentieth century. In culture, reductionism grew not from a rational path toward specialization but in response to the impending threat of humanity's weapons used against ourselves. In the aftermath of two World Wars, artists began to articulate the culture's dramatic loss of humanity. For many, Hiroshima and Nagasaki revealed the naïveté of earlier attempts to capture beauty via canvas or concert hall. In movements like Dadaism and Abstract Expressionism, artists created images that visualized trauma, disillusionment, and dehumanization and attempted to counter it not with beauty but with irony or the pure power of expressive gestures. The resulting work, an honest depiction of our loss, screams at us with contempt for a dehumanized view of life.

At the same time, artists recognized the gap left by the weakening witness of the church in culture and increasingly came to see themselves as secular prophets and priests with a call to "speak the truth" against the "establishment." They intentionally isolated themselves from society and produced work aimed at shocking people into recognizing and decrying the horrors of the age. As critic Robert Hughes has noted, "the shock of the new" became a way of life in the twentieth century modernist experiment.

Artists like Marcel Duchamp, Mark Rothko, and Ad Reinhardt point to a world in which art is no longer decoration or representation of historical events. By creating a new language to speak into society, they began to express an artistic via negativa, an artistic version of the Christian theological and philosophical tradition that points to truth by emphasizing what truth is not. These artists created an aesthetic antithesis against a direct link of art as power (Duchamp), depicting the angst of the "edge" of our time and space (Rothko), and pursuing the purity of our sensory experiences to see beyond representation (Reinhardt).

During this period, the voices of artists became more and more esoteric and elitist. Their work was generative, providing ways for viewers to confront the dehumanized world. But at the same time, a reductionist vision began to solidify (especially among the critics), so that artists' confrontational nature and insistence on defining themselves against the status quo resulted only in ideological fragmentation and marginalization. Even the new ideals that they had for art—for the purity and unity of expression—made little contact with the lives of most people in their culture.

The gap between artists and the wider society has only widened since the rise of the culture wars and the increasingly overt use of art in that struggle. All artists have been conscripted by progressive draft boards as frontline soldiers to defend "freedom of expression" against tradition and conformity. It is a disturbing irony that freedom of expression and the diversity of artistic voices have been early casualties. Artists have been pressed—sometimes willingly and sometimes not—to speak not for their own work, vision, and principles but for (usually leftist) ideologies. The implicit and explicit cultural pressures for ideological uniformity are so high that one could say that in the culture wars artists are free to express anything *other* than beauty.

As the ideals faded, what was left was commercialism. Think of Andy Warhol's Pop art featuring Marilyn Monroe and Campbell's soup cans. He was brilliant in capturing the "icons" of his age with an exquisite touch and personal flair. But though his own works were generative, providing an important conversation and an enduring legacy, his Pop works led to thousands of derivative works, flooding the market. With the exception of ideological uses, today's art has been commoditized to such an extent that we often see commerce as the prevailing goal of art, and value the arts only as transactional tools to achieve fame and thus wealth.

The shock of the new has devolved to a game of gaining the "fifteen minutes of fame" that Warhol forecast each of us will someday have. In our river metaphor, the artists are struggling in polluted waters to find the oxygen they need to create. Artists are adaptable, but to survive in a stressed ecosystem like ours, that often means becoming "bottom-feeders" like catfish, feeding off the bottom layers of culture, and the pollution there turns many into monstrous, hideous creatures. Their creativity is given over to survival—and those who are fittest to survive are usually those who fashion the cleverest means to twist and adapt to the celebrity model of art. Too often, they create primarily what they think will sell. Speaking recently to a group of musicians, I implored them not to do so. "Be a trout, instead," I said. "Endeavor to go upstream into the tributaries and find clear, pure waters. Create upstream, and then what you create will affect the whole stream."

But the problem for them, and for me, is that today no pure waters are to be found upstream either. Thus, a key Culture Care strategy, as we will see later, is to create diverse microcosms of pure water so that "trout" can survive in our cultural ecosystem.

We are living in a time of cultural upheaval. No matter what field an artist operates in, the sustainability of art that points us beyond ourselves is threatened. Every sphere is being shaken up. Galleries have faced a frozen market since the Lehman shock of 2008. Every mid-tier gallery in New York's Chelsea neighborhood now struggles to pay rent. The music industry is no longer able to give lucrative contracts to musicians because every song is now worth 99 cents. Top modern dancers have to pay for rehearsal space out of their own pockets. Publishers, threatened by the lower margins of Amazon and electronic books, are offering less and less rewarding contracts to writers. Even established first-rate writers cannot count on being given a New York City reading today because it is not worth the risk for the publisher.

We could be facing a public eclipse of those species called art, dance, and music. (Poetry is the only field that seems to be producing at a terrific pace at the moment, partly because poets do not depend on commercial forces to keep writing. But not many of us seem to be *reading* poetry.) The arts audience is changing and shrinking amid an ever-demanding chorus of offers online that change how we assess the value of an experience.

Why is Culture Care needed? From the perspective of the arts, it is because today, an artist cannot simply paint; a novelist cannot simply write; a pianist cannot simply play. Utilitarian pragmatism and commercialism so thoroughly pervade culture that without some shift in worldview and expectation, what we do as artists—the activities of the arts—will be neither sustainable nor generative. We will not be able to resist their use as weapons in the culture wars.

We need to recognize our time as a genesis moment.

From Culture Wars to a Common Life

The cultural fragmentation we have experienced, and the reductionism that has accompanied minute categorization within all disciplines, have contributed directly to today's polarized ideological positions. Too many of us live isolated—sometimes more literally, sometimes virtually—with the tribes on our own cultural islands. We have no meaningful engagement with or understanding of the human beings across the divide. Few people are able or willing to build bridges. When we are living in a mode of survival and scarcity rather than generativity, we easily fall into viewing those outside as "enemies" locked in utter competition for commodities or power that should be ours.

Sociologist James Davison Hunter noted more than twenty years ago that participants in culture wars employ language that reduces the "enemy" to a caricature, portraying their ideas as not only false but pernicious, and alienating their humanity. Hunter identifies the culprit in *Culture Wars* (1991), arguing that a shared weakness "in both orthodox and progressivist alliances" is "an implicit yet imperious disregard for the goal of a common life."

This "disregard for the goal of a common life" is the abject failure of our times; but from this failure we can begin a new path toward Culture Care.

Culture is not a territory to be won or lost but a resource we are called to steward with care. *Culture is a garden to be cultivated.*

I have seen this type of care modeled. From 2003 to 2009, I served on the National Council on the Arts, advising National Endowment for the Arts chair Dana Gioia. He often stated that "the NEA is the

Poland of the culture wars: everyone wants to fight on her turf, but no one cares about her inhabitants." Gioia, who is one of our leading poets, has also been a business executive. His approach to culture drew from both standpoints, including bringing disciplined management to the agency. While I served on the Council, I saw him work diligently to build consensus around caring for our culture. I saw that it is possible for a political leader in Washington to work toward the common good.

But all too often politicians and political factions take an easier path, picking on the arts as instigators of cultural ills. Few make the effort to care for culture. Few acknowledge in artists the potential and opportunity to help us express our deepest longings for a free and humane society.

After many years of culture wars, no one can claim victory. We have all been further dehumanized, fragmented, and exiled from genuine conversation. Culture at large is a polluted, over-commoditized system that has failed all of us.

Certainly, ideas are worth defending and fighting for, but we have now come to a point where even the core principles of contemporary ideologies have been compromised. The language of both liberalism and conservatism has been truncated and distorted, and this dysfunction is dismantling the language of culture. We need mediation in culture to help bridge the divide—not so much to broker an agreement about what we believe as to communicate beyond our differences.

Is there an alternative to the ongoing starvation or pollution of our cultural soul? How can we step back from a utilitarian or commercial posture toward the arts and culture? When we commit to Culture Care, one of the things we commit to is moving beyond poisoned language and the "imperious disregard" for the life of those unlike ourselves that Hunter notes. Culture Care emphasizes the common good.

Constructive cultural work begins not in opposition but in sharing: of ideals generously argued, of visions for future generations, of opportunities to meet and dialogue with the other—all of which could occur in the context of the arts and from there mirrored into society. From this point, Culture Care can and will lead to rigorous debate—debate that is premised not in defending homogeneous ideological "tribes" but in ways to care for the whole of culture and all of its participants.

Approached this way, we can perhaps redeem the ideals for the artist in culture that the elites of the prior century could only show by negation. Artists and their friends (hopefully including their friends in the churches) may now be uniquely positioned to break the malaise of the current polarization and develop a truly prophetic stance toward culture. It will require acting not just for shock and self-aggrandizement but for cultivation and common flourishing. Artists can become known instead as "citizen artists," who lead in society with their imagination and their work.[3]

Artists can admit to the failure of the culture wars stance and abandon it, creating instead opportunities for genesis moments in culture, moments in which dialogue can happen, in which caricatures can be discarded, and in which deeper concerns can be addressed. Artists can take the lead in the generosity of such dialogues, providing opportunities and creating microcosms of true diversity. And finally, to be consistent with the "three G's" of Culture Care, artists can think generationally, to provide for a stronger foundation for deeper reflections in culture.

T. S. Eliot writes helpfully of just such a deeper view—of a common life and the common good, in fact—in *Notes Towards the Definition of Culture* (1948):

---

3   Listen, for example, to an interview with artist Dario Robleto (www.onbeing.org/program/dario-robleto-sculptor-of-memory/6640).

If we take culture seriously, we see that a people does not need merely enough to eat but a proper and particular cuisine.... Culture may even be described simply as that which makes life worth living.

Today, "what makes life worth living" for artists is a dying ember. And bullet holes in our schools and high rates of suicide for sensitive populations like teenagers remind us that cultural failure is no abstract question. Casualties are mounting. Amy Winehouse, Philip Seymour Hoffman, Robin Williams, to name a few from a sadly long list.

It was only a few years ago that I asked, "What happened to the young woman with the operatic voice, a vibrant part of her church community, who stepped confidently onto the stage at the 1986 Grammy Awards. When we see Whitney Houston's life, her struggles, and her death played out in front of us, we shudder and lament. But how much of her journey is predicated on our own consumption of culture, a culture littered with the discarded bodies of gifted individuals?" Now Whitney Houston's shocking death just before the 2012 Grammy Awards is only an afterthought in a growing list of celebrity artists prematurely lost to us.

We have done little to cultivate the soil of culture for the next generation, so efforts we make now to plant seeds of culture will likely not yield significant results for some time. This is a bleak assessment, but it may be encouraging to reflect on parallels in the natural world: volcanic soil is highly fertile, and forest fires can benefit the ecosystem. The right conditions and care make rapid regeneration possible in the aftermath of many disasters.

Generative activity is transformative. But living into the ideal of a common life will demand much from each artist—and much from each of us in other spheres of influence. Destruction and dissolution is far easier than creation and connection. We need vision, courage, and perseverance. This is why the care and cultivation of culture begins with the care and cultivation of the soul.

Soul Care

We have just noted how artists have in recent years been pushed to the margins, where many have resorted to various efforts to shock or transgress to get attention. I have often noticed that when these same artists are placed in an environment of nurture, such as an arts residency, what they create has a different tone. These thoughts came together recently while I was considering Culture Care values, and I realized that much of what I speak of here flows out of conversations with my wife. Culture Care principles are based in part on the therapeutic language I have heard my wife use in describing her work. That language of *care* is an extension of her bringing home that bouquet of flowers to care for our souls.

As a psychotherapist, Judy does not expect her clients to come in happy and smiling. Her clients come because they need help. At some level they are aware of the fragmentation that is disrupting their lives. My wife assumes that her clients will arrive upset, angry, and dysfunctional. She sees it as her work to help heal the wounds—and to do so she listens carefully and gives the clients their own work to do under her guidance.

Similarly, if our prevailing culture is wounded and dysfunctional, should we not expect that most cultural artifacts will speak of the ills of the world? Cultural catalyst Erwin McManus tells the story of a conversation he had with a young artist who was struggling to avoid making art to be used for propaganda. He wanted to create works that expressed authentic emotions. But the only emotions this artist thought of as authentic were negative—"anger, betrayal, fear." He had never thought to ask whether love or happiness could be true human experiences that could be portrayed with authenticity. And he was unable to connect with what makes life worth living (both figuratively and, sadly, literally).[4]

When we hear primarily of alienation and suffering, the temptation to despair is strong. But if we can listen carefully while holding on to hope, honest assessments of our cultural problems can point us to discoveries of self-awareness—including the recognition of innate longings that we have been attempting to satisfy in unhealthy ways— that can in turn lead to healing.

There are thus significant overlaps for Culture Care not only with Creation Care but with Soul Care, which is the spiritual development and psychological integration that can result when we diligently follow good guidance. The work of Soul Care, the work of both therapist and client, is extemporaneous. It cannot be linear but is rather an interactive and creative process that responds on an ongoing basis to the shifting needs of the soul. All effective care providers are in this sense artists of the soul.

One way to envisage Culture Care at work is to transpose our knowledge of mental health and spiritual formation to culture. Most people cannot escape dysfunction on their own, and untended emotional wounds are more likely to fester than to heal. On one hand, it is the job of the psychotherapist to map a path toward healing for the client, not to leave a hurting person fragmented, stuck along the journey, or trapped in perpetual dependency on therapy. But at the same time, psychological and emotional health—like spiritual growth—cannot be imposed from the outside. This is also true for culture.

One of the ways that people who have experienced traumatizing events begin to find healing from symptoms like flashbacks and nightmares is by learning to retell the story of their traumatic encounters in a safe environment. This helps them move from involuntarily re-experiencing the emotional pain of the event to connecting the memory with supportive listeners and a larger framework of meaning.

4 Erwin Raphael McManus, *The Artisan Soul*, HarperOne, 2014, p. 33–34.

It helps them see the trauma as one episode in their larger life story rather than as defining their identity.

Similarly, Culture Care starts with the identification and articulation of brokenness. It creates a safe space for truth-telling. But it does not stop there. It starts with listening and then invites people onward toward beauty, wholeness, and healing. As we become able to acknowledge the truth of our situation and can tell that story, we are encouraged to move into caring for artists and all other participants in the culture, into creating contexts for deeper conversation, into fostering spiritual growth, and sometimes into problem-solving.

A key reason that I connect Culture Care with Judy's work in Soul Care is that our experience of beauty depends on more than intellectual and technical accomplishments.

On an aesthetic level, learning to perceive deeper depths of beauty includes training or apprenticeship in the craft and tradition in which we are participating. A viewer may need to be shown how to open up him or herself to certain forms of beauty, or to be trained in how to read a painting. A listener may need instruction in hearing tone and color in a symphony. A student may need to be trained to approach an object from different perspectives. A child or novice may need to be exposed to many instances of what others have recognized as beautiful before being able to form a coherent judgment. And of course anyone working in the arts will have to practice diligently.

But beyond this, our very state of being affects our ability both to perceive and to create beauty. If we doubt that beauty exists, for example, we will have a truncated experience even when we encounter it. And as I found in New York, it is possible to reach the point of rejecting beauty as ephemeral, saccharine, or naïve and viewing its pursuit as archaic, unfashionable, or déclassé.

Appreciation of the depths of beauty is a condition of our physical, mental, and spiritual health—and of our physical, mental, emotional, relational, and spiritual maturity. We all begin immature and unformed. We all bear some degree of disorder. And we all bear a degree of responsibility to address this disorder. There is a saying that you cannot share what you do not have. Similarly, our maturity sets a limit on the quality and expressiveness of the work we can produce.

We often think of our great artists, musicians, and writers—those who have demonstrated the ability to express beauty—as great souls. Most or all of them faced, and many overcame, great disorder; we will encounter a few of their stories in the coming chapters. Wesley Hill, a professor at Trinity School for Ministry, recently told a story (it may be a legend) about a Yale student working under the great Old Testament scholar Brevard Childs. The student was unhappy with his grade and asked how he could improve his next essay. Childs replied, "Become a deeper person."[5]

How can we do this? Certainly not in isolation. In psychological terms, we need to do the work, to follow the path toward healing that is mapped out for us. This might include finding healthy people to emulate or safe spaces in which to incubate new expressions of creativity. It may involve imaginative exercises to extend empathy and combat narcissism. In spiritual terms, we need to respond in faith and take hold of the grace we are so freely given. This might include taking advantage of spiritual directors—personal trainers for the soul—or embracing some regimen of spiritual exercises and practical disciplines to build spiritual and moral muscles and bring order to our souls.

Soul Care will require nurturing spaces for such formation—but I see these looking less like celebrity rehab clinics and more like working neighborhood gyms or Olympic training centers. Such spaces would feature purposeful, visionary leadership by active mentors and trainers committed to Culture Care. In each space, a community of peers would gather to work together and challenge each other to

5 Wesley Hill, commenting on a post at wesleyhill.tumblr.com, July 10, 2014.

excellence and growth to prepare themselves for competition and collaboration. This is a theme to which we will return.

A healthy and thriving culture is impossible without the participation of artists and other leaders who are educated intellectually, trained experientially, formed spiritually, and growing morally. Beauty is both a goal and a catalyst for each of these elements.

Beauty as Food
for the Soul

Once we see the connection of Culture Care with Soul Care, the next set of questions to ask becomes clear: What are we inviting people into? What sort of food does the soul need? What is beauty, and how does it feed that part of us that is more than instinct and appetite? How might beauty address personal and cultural fragmentation and dysfunction?

These questions have captivated people throughout recorded history, and those trying to tease out answers usually find themselves in deep and sometimes murky waters. Beauty is notoriously hard to pin down, and it is often spoken of together with other ultimate concerns, particularly the true and the good. Dallas Willard has even defined beauty as "goodness made manifest to the senses."[6]

How deeply intertwined these three core qualities are is debated, but experience shows that a lack of either truth or goodness (whether in quality of workmanship or in the moral sense) detracts from the beauty of a given artifact. Similarly, a lack of attention to beauty in presenting a truth hampers its appeal and adoption. And we have just discussed ways that a culture that downplays the pursuit of beauty also loses its appetite for truth and goodness.

If beauty is food for the soul, we can also think in terms of the many things we are still learning about the interaction between food choices and the health of body, mind, and spirit. When we are busy or distracted, it is easy to fall back on eating overly processed "convenience" foods. Their empty calories do little to strengthen our bodies and may indeed create unhealthy appetites or increase our

6   Quoted in John Ortberg, "Dallas Willard, a Man from Another 'Time Zone'," *Christianity Today Online* (christianitytoday.com), May 8, 2013.

vulnerability to clinical depression. When feeding our souls, we dare not substitute surface attraction—that which is effortlessly appreciated and soon exhausted of virtue—for true beauty. Instead we need to cultivate the appetite for the best soul food, whole and unprocessed, requiring time to absorb and digest.

Much more can and should be said on this theme, but for now it will be helpful instead to draw together the threads implicit in our discussion so far and offer a working definition of beauty to ground our work in Culture Care:

Beauty is the quality connected with those things that are in themselves *appealing* and desirable. Beautiful things are a *delight* to the senses, a *pleasure* to the mind, and a *refreshment* for the spirit. Beauty *invites* us in, capturing our attention and making us want to linger. Beautiful things are *worth* our scrutiny, rewarding to contemplate, deserving of pursuit. They inspire—or even demand—a response, whether sharing them in community or acting to extend their beauty into other spheres.

Beauty may not be embodied in an enduring form—a given bouquet of flowers will soon wilt, though a painting or poem can last for generations—but it is something we want to remember and something we would not want to change. Beauty is thus connected with *satisfaction*—which may point to the way beauty feeds the soul.

Beauty touches on some combination of qualities—difficult to quantify—of pattern, design, form, shape, color, sound, light, integrity, and relationship. It appeals to us at multiple levels, speaking to our intellect and our logical capacities as well as our emotions and spirits. While it is commonly connected more with our physical senses and the material world than with the world of ideas, people often appeal to beauty when talking about the pursuit of knowledge, and the best scientific and mathematical theories are called beautiful in their simplicity or elegance.

So far this definition is not controversial and could be embraced by people across a wide spectrum of belief. Let me next sketch out four important themes about beauty for Culture Care. These are gratuity, stewardship, justice, and our response.

A Christian understanding of beauty begins with the recognition that God does not *need* us, or the creation. Beauty is a gratuitous gift of the creator God; it finds its source and its purpose in God's character. God, out of his gratuitous love, created a world he did not need because he is an Artist.

Beauty itself is not, in this sense, necessary. Sometimes it seems as if many people in the modern age have attempted to prove this point negatively—like modernist architects and city planners doing their best to demonstrate that any object that could be made beautifully could also be made without beauty.

But even if we would agree that beauty is not necessary to our daily survival, it is still necessary for our flourishing. Our sense of beauty and our creativity are central to what it means to be made in the image of a creative God. The satisfaction in beauty we feel is connected deeply with our reflection of God's character to create and value gratuity. It is part of our human nature. This is why our soul hungers for beauty.

Because it is gratuitous, beauty points beyond itself, beyond survival to satisfaction. We think of it in opposition to narrowness, scarcity, drudgery, and constraint. We think instead of what is expansive, generous, abundant, connected, and expressive. Beauty also connects us with the *why* of living. It points to discoveries waiting to be made about the creation. It points toward questions of right relationships, of ultimate meaning, and even of eternity. It points backward and outward and forward to our ultimate Source and Sustainer.

When we encounter beauty, we want to slow down and partake of its refreshment, to let it reorient us to our deepest longings and reconnect us to our deepest selves. And however undeveloped or distorted it is, it is our innate sense of beauty that makes us struggle in the face of the utilitarian pressures of modernism, even when we cannot express ourselves and our longings in words.

In its gratuity and generosity, beauty—paradoxically—helps set boundaries on how we live. Our actions can be assessed on whether or not they lead toward beauty. We can be challenged by comparisons of our work with works that reveal a higher standard. This may explain why many modernists overtly resist the very concept of beauty.

In pushing back against modernism, it may also be helpful to introduce an idea from the philosopher Roger Scruton. He defines beauty in part as that which repays contemplation for its own sake, and claims that beauty and utility only conflict in the short run. Beauty may not be "practical," but he has noted that when people neglect beauty they produce, ultimately, useless things. Focusing on mere function actually will consign an object to oblivion. Beauty, he says, is what makes things last.[7]

I said earlier that beauty is a gift that we discover, receive, and *steward*. This is a claim that beauty is found both in nature and in culture. It is something that is given to us, and it is also something we human beings can add to—something we can cultivate.

God asks us to continue as he began. We have the ability and responsibility to create more (gratuitous) beauty. J. R. R. Tolkien, author of *The Lord of the Rings*, used the helpful concept of sub-creation.[8] In anything we make, we bring our creative energies, but we are always acting in stewardship of something that we have been given. At our best, we work *with* our "raw" materials, honoring their properties and respecting their limits, not working against the grain or twisting them out of context. In short, we need to love both nature and culture to exercise a proper stewardship.

---

7   Roger Scruton, lecture at the University Club, Washington, DC, December 1, 2009.
8   J. R. R. Tolkien, "On Fairy Stories," in *The Tolkien Reader*. New York: Ballantine Books, 1966, p. 58.

Recent thinking in agriculture offers some ideas that may transfer to the stewardship of culture. Localism acknowledges the unique character of each region and suggests that it is a good to grow produce that is native to our place and in tune with the climate, the natural soil, and the local botany. Hothouse flowers or imported vegetables may be desirable when our local climate is inhospitable or some disaster has damaged local crops, but there is a virtue in local produce. It often tastes better. Eating locally seasonal foods seems to be better for our bodies.

Effective stewardship leads to generative work and a generative culture. We turn wheat to bread—and bread into community. We turn grapes to wine—and wine into occasions for joyful camaraderie, conviviality, conversation, and creativity. We turn minerals into paints—and paints to works that lift the heart or stir the spirit. We turn ideas and experiences into imaginative worlds for sheer enjoyment and to expand the scope of our empathy.

As in Creation Care, cultural stewardship includes trying to find our place in the wider ecosystem. It asks us to consider what we have been given and where we are situated. It will take human nature into account—acknowledging our true longings and limitations.

Another contemporary philosopher, Elaine Scarry, is known for connecting beauty with justice. Dr. Scarry spoke at the spring 2002 IAM conference at New York University, co-sponsored by *Image Journal* and titled, audaciously at the time, "The Return of Beauty" (after September 11, beauty was much needed, and it seemed to return as a value to the contemporary art world).

One point of connection between the beauty and justice, she says, is that "beauty, sooner or later, brings us into contact with our own capacity for making errors."[9] I resonate with Dr. Scarry's observation. An encounter with beauty can open the door of perception to turn from our errors and begin a journey toward the authentic. What

9   Elaine Scarry, *On Beauty and Being Just*, Princeton University Press, 1999, p. 31.

Christians call "repentance"—from the Greek *metanoia*, to turn back—is often sparked by an encounter with the beautiful.

Ultimately, the reality of beauty led to my own journey to faith. The link between beauty, justice, and our necessary response is a key value of Culture Care, but it was only while writing this book that I have become able to recognize and start to articulate it. That single gesture of generosity, the reminder of beauty in my life by Judy, opened a journey of exploration that led my "falling into" faith in Christ.

My own failure to value beauty and to acknowledge it as a need for my life and my art led to many more struggles. I speak of this in several other writings, but the more I experienced beauty, especially the beauty that was being created through my own hands, the more alienated I felt from it. I did not have a model or category in which to receive beauty. It was only through my encounter of "seeing" Christ and his sacrifice in love for me, through the reading of *Jerusalem*, William Blake's last epic poem (1804), that I saw the *beauty of sacrifice* in Christ.

I said earlier that Jesus is the source of beauty. As that source, Jesus is appealing, and knowing him brings delight—an assertion with consequences for the activities and approaches of every individual and community that reflects Jesus, not least the church.

My encounter with Christ's beauty, reflected in the Isaiah 61 passages I shared earlier, has resulted in a series of shifts in how I view myself and the role of art in society. What I write here is the direct result of my own *metanoia*, a journey that was nourished by Judy's act of generosity.

It will be helpful at this point to consider the goals that I have come to recognize in the years since I received that bouquet. What is it to which we should aspire as artists and creative catalysts (those who may not consider themselves artists but are still key cultural players)?

We can turn again here to the Isaiah 61 passage. In the same verse that talks about a crown of beauty, the prophet makes an explicit connection between beauty, suffering, and justice that speaks directly to a role the arts should be playing. Those who receive crowns of beauty are those who have been poor, broken-hearted, captive, mourning, grieving, and despairing—and the result of God's intervention is that these same people are to "be called oaks of righteousness." Part of the good news they hear is a work order. The purpose of the prophet's message—which Jesus says that he fulfills— is a call to act for justice and renewal.

Those who have suffered are the very ones who

... will rebuild the ancient ruins
and restore the places long devastated;
they will renew the ruined cities
that have been devastated for generations (Isaiah 61:3b–4, NIV)

Even those who are still considering Jesus' claims will find a grounding for justice work in the cultivation of beauty. An encounter with beauty can show us what could be, and can make us rightly dissatisfied with the way things are. In the face of the undeniable and often unbearable human suffering all around us, we must still affirm beauty and work to make our culture reflect it. This is why a Culture Care approach will encourage the truth-telling of alienation, suffering, and oppression alongside the truth-telling of justice, hope, and restoration.

Certainly, some or all of our roles should aim to surprise our jaded culture with delight and remind our fellows of what we humans truly long for. Artists in the last century have been functioning in society to reveal brokenness; in this century, can they lead the way toward reconnection, reconciliation, and reintegration?

In addition to the ideas above, a framework for beauty should also include the notion of sacrifice. Beauty, as poets in Japan saw a long time ago, is connected with death. The Japanese ideogram for beauty (美) is made up of two ideograms, the one for sheep (羊) laid on top of the one for large (大).

Apparently in China, where the ideograms originated, what was beautiful was a "fat sheep." In a culture in which eating meat is a rare occurrence, a fat sheep was supreme delight. But in Japan, a deeper connection was made to the sacrifice of the sheep.

Sacrifices are needed to provide beauty in the world. In the following chapters, we will look at some roles through which these sacrifices might take place, roles that depend on the care and feeding of the soul. We will look at a new model for leadership as border care—building bridges and serving as messengers or ambassadors to separated groups, trying to find a way to the common good. We will look at language care, finding trade languages and a generative grammar to defuse the culture wars. And we will look at various ways of stewardship of the wider ecosystem of our culture, including the cultivation of artists and business leaders who can be the custodians of culture.

Leadership from the Margins

Earlier I noted that artists have been pushed to the margins. Recently I was speaking with my colleague and collaborator Bruce Herman. He introduced me to an Old English word used in *Beowulf*: *mearcstapas*, translated "border-walkers" or "border-stalkers."[10] In the tribal realities of earlier times, these were individuals who lived on the edges of their groups, going in and out of them, sometimes bringing back news to the tribe.

Artists are instinctively uncomfortable in homogeneous groups, and in "border-stalking" we have a role that both addresses the reality of fragmentation and also offers a fitting means by which artists can help people from all our many and divided cultural tribes learn to appreciate the margins, lower barriers to understanding and communication, and start to defuse the culture wars. Artists on the margins of various groups can be deputized (not conscripted) to represent tribal identities while still being messengers of hope and reconciliation to a divided culture.

Part of the role can be thought of in the terms of Soul Care. A psychotherapist, as an artist of the soul, needs to know the "tribal" reality that her clients are facing. In some sense, a broken marriage is due the unresolved tension of two tribal identities, but all marriages are "cross-cultural," so a good therapist will help raise to the surface the issues and resources of each culture in the relationship, and then help the two conflicting cultures come together as complements. Marriage counseling happens in a generally trusting context where the husband and wife are both responding to the guidance of the therapist. But at a community level, and particularly when the tribes

10 *Mearcstapa* is one of the several terms used to describe Grendel. See this helpful essay: "Beowulf and the Anglo-Saxon Mark: Borders, Transgression, and Grendel's Arm." *Sententiae, The Harvard Undergraduate Journal of Medieval Sciences*, June 2, 2011 (harvardsententiae.org).

in conflict have not asked for a guide, a would-be societal therapist faces a deeply challenging task.

Mearcstapa is not a comfortable role. Life on the borders of a group—and in the space between groups—is prone to dangers literal and figurative, with people both at "home" and among the "other" likely to misunderstand or mistrust the motivations, piety, and loyalty of the border-stalker. But *mearcstapa* can be a role of cultural leadership in a new mode, serving functions including empathy, memory, warning, guidance, mediation, and reconciliation. Those who journey to the borders of their group and beyond will encounter new vistas and knowledge that can enrich the group.

In *The Lord of the Rings*, J. R. R. Tolkien introduces the shadowy figure of Strider the Ranger at an inn in the homely village of Bree, where the comfortable and hospitable innkeeper warns the travelers not to trust him. Strider is a *mearcstapa*, and it is in large part his ability to move in and out of tribes and boundaries that makes him an indispensable guide and protector and that helps him become an effective leader, fulfilling his destiny as Aragorn, High King of Gondor and Arnor, uniting two kingdoms. He even marries across tribes with his union to Arwen, daughter of Elrond Half-Elven.

Often artists are branded as "difficult people" in society, hard to pin down and notorious for being independent. In Tolkien's story, the travelers only accept Strider as a guide when they receive a letter that vouches for him. But Strider might speak for many artists in his comment to his reluctant new friends: " 'But I must admit,' he added with a queer laugh, 'that I hoped you would take to me for my own sake. A hunted man sometimes wearies of distrust and longs for friendship.' "[11]

I am giving the name *mearcstapa* to a role that many artists and others have come to naturally. Many more who might thrive in this role go through life with their potential untapped or misused. But the leadership quality that lurks within them is too valuable to be dismissed or left dormant. Identifying and befriending those

---

11   J. R. R. Tolkien, *The Lord of the Rings: The Fellowship of the Ring.* Ballantine, [1965] 1973, p. 232.

with this gifting, many of whom may start out awkward or ill-fitting, is critical to Culture Care. But to come to full maturity, a *mearcstapa* will need not only friendship but deliberate cultivation in community. Tolkien understood this; he tells us later in the story that Strider is supported in his role by other Rangers and had lived for many years training with the elves of Rivendell and Lórien.

Artists who come to embrace the role of *mearcstapa* and find support and training to walk it out can become leaders that make possible the reunification of divided kingdoms; they can be reconcilers of division and fragmentation. They can release great generativity and flourishing.

In the story of the Good Samaritan Jesus tells in Luke 10, we see a man who is considered by the listeners as "other" and "enemy" giving generous help to an injured man when religious professionals and the respected members of his own tribe fail him. Artists have a great capacity to see someone who is "other" as their "neighbor" in the sense that Jesus defines this role in the parable. They can follow his instruction to "do likewise" in showing mercy and making full recovery possible.

Where does this openness to the "other" come from in artists? Some may grow out of empathy earned because artists are themselves often exiled from a normative tribal identity. There is also training to extend that empathy. In art, we constantly train ourselves to inhabit or portray the "other." Artists learn to be adaptable and blend into an environment while not belonging to it, which also requires learning to speak new tribal languages.

This is an area with real dangers and real opportunities. Sometimes artists lose their connection with their original tribe and their core identity in adapting to a new environment. (I mentioned earlier Whitney Houston's struggles with success. Her case is all too common—though her legacy also includes many generative elements.) But if adaptability can be exercised without sacrificing one's core beliefs and ideological convictions, the experience will actually deepen such convictions. It will also mark a path toward a more perceptive and wider-scale view of culture.

The generosity of an artist in this sense can mean mediation in the culture wars, beginning by overcoming caricatures and injecting diversity, nuance, and even paradox into the nature of the conversation, and then moving on even to teach society a language of empathy and reconciliation. Grounded artists can provide rallying points around which reconciliation can begin. Through such practices, they can become "good Samaritans" to a divided culture. Let's explore some fictional and biographical cases.

'Tell 'em about the Dream!'

"You never really understand a person," Atticus Finch tells us in *To Kill a Mockingbird*, "until you consider things from his point of view ... until you climb into his skin and walk around in it."

In the story we see Atticus's little daughter "Scout" running through the streets of Maycomb, Alabama chasing her brother, Jem, and her friend, Dill. "Maycomb County had recently been told that it had nothing to fear but fear itself," recalls Scout. There is an eye-of-the-storm stillness in the streets; slow, ambling folks who "shuffled in and out of the stores" and "took their time about everything. A day was twenty-four hours long but seemed longer."[12] The Great Depression has gripped the county, and the country had been deeply wounded by World War I. There were more conflicts to come.

Harper Lee's classic work brings the reader into the heart of that American struggle via an inquisitive, feisty, creative girl. Scout is a *mearcstapa* in the story, learning to lurk in and out of tribal identities divided by race. And Lee was herself working as a *mearcstapa* by writing to evoke empathy for all sides of the divide. *To Kill a Mockingbird* was published in 1960. Harper Lee remembered her country-lawyer father, and in the character of Atticus Finch she translated the principles of justice and equality he taught her into great art. Lee set out to tell what she called a "simple love story," but the result was a powerful catalyst to transform a cultural mindset from bigotry to respect for human dignity.

Her art reshaped the world. Former Supreme Court Justice Sandra Day O'Connor, for example, has said the book made her want to become a lawyer. The book also foreshadows Martin Luther King,

12 Harper Lee, *To Kill a Mockingbird*. Grand Central Publishing, 1988 [1960], p. 6.

Jr.'s "I Have a Dream" speech—and anticipated it by three years. I see it as one of the twentieth century's great cultural artifacts for wrestling with issues of humanity and as a model to teach us how to speak with empathic creativity and transform the cultural river.

Atticus Finch is defending Tom Robinson, a man falsely accused of rape. Knowing that the town is conspiring to lynch him, Atticus "sits guard" in front of the jailhouse where Mr. Robinson is being held. He sets up a chair and reading light outside the cell window, creating a borderline. He is using a theatrical prop to make his case, if you will—bringing his living room right the heart of the conflict. Creating this borderline and acknowledging the division is essential for reconciliation.

A mob gathers. Scout, Jem, and Dill walk right into that circle, making Atticus quite nervous. Scout then recognizes a face in the crowd: "Don't you remember me, Mr. Cunningham? I'm Jean Louise Finch. You brought us some hickory nuts one time, remember? ... I go to school with Walter ... he is your boy, ain't he? Ain't he, Sir?"[13]

Scout remembered that "Atticus had said it was the polite thing to talk to people about what they were interested in, not about what you were interested in."[14] Atticus had taught her empathy. So she speaks to Mr. Cunningham using a big word Atticus taught her: "entailment." Mr. Cunningham had brought the hickory nuts to Atticus in thanks for work Atticus had performed for the Cunningham family. Now Scout reminds Mr. Cunningham about entailment, or a swap of one work for another. It becomes a code to unlock his humanity, to help him remember. Scout also uses it to tap into his conscience, his awareness of how human beings should treat each other, with dignity and respect. And she defuses the situation, in her determined innocence. Both Atticus and Scout bring a sense of humanity into the divide; and both are willing to be "border-stalkers," communicating intentionally across boundaries.

---

13 Ibid, p. 205.
14 Ibid.

Our culture has made progress of a sort since Harper Lee first wrote. Just as our views on pollution have changed, now a racial lynch mob is practically unthinkable. But some things do not change. Every age seems to find its own "other." The temptation to dispense a rough "justice" against some individual or group flares up whenever we lose our focus on our common humanity and succumb to fear.

Just like the mob in front of Tom Robinson's jail cell, our culture is still prone to create scapegoats, dodging our own culpability and responsibility over cultural or systemic problems by blaming them on innocent individuals or groups. We still blind ourselves to the dehumanizing forces this unleashes. For any given provocation, we are egged on by our instant, omnipresent media to unleash our basest instincts—we might think of them as cultural "fight-flight-freeze" responses—rather than committing ourselves to the slower process of seeking truth.[15] (One genuinely new thing is the virtual mob, which can be just as inhumane and culturally damaging as any physical mob.)

This self-debasement of our humanity in desperate and irrational fear of the "other" is a result of poor cultural stewardship. Little wonder that our culture is still bedeviled by cynicism, apathy, and anger. Cycles of violence and revenge are an ongoing reality. And when we focus on headlines and newsfeeds, we come to expect more of the same.

How would—how do—we respond when faced with an angry mob ready to commit an atrocity against us or some "other"? Would we want to fight back, fire against fire, hatred against hatred? Scout offers a better model. She does not even confront bigotry by arguing for justice. What she does in her naiveté is to step into the mob and remind people that they are her neighbors. She *becomes* a bouquet of flowers in the heart of conflict.

Reminding people of our common life—that we are neighbors first—is a task of Culture Care. We acknowledge openly the borders of our

---

15 Many Christians respond similarly to cultural artifacts, focusing on surface offenses rather than going deep enough to see truths.

groups, and acknowledge too the legitimate things that divide us. Our responsibility, then, is to re-humanize this divide. An emphasis on our role as *neighbor* as part of our identity begins this process by reminding us of our shared cultural and geographical spaces and the fact that proximity brings responsibility. Even apart from Jesus' call to love our neighbor, we know that our common flourishing depends on each other.

Scout defuses the situation by being fully human, fully a child. What she does naively, we must do courageously. Reconcilers of culture must speak like children, which is to say innocent of pretense and full of determined hope, confident in our own experience of beauty and joy in life, connected with the highest potential and calling of our common humanity, and expectant of finding this good in the lives of others.

Our arts and conversations should point toward beauty and healing. When they do, we may remind our neighbors, and ourselves, of who we are and who we can be when we exercise our capacity for empathy, gratitude, and generosity. This language of empathy is truly generative, and it is just as surprising in a cynical culture as is Scout's presence to the mob in the story. When such an unexpected voice breaks in, it can defuse culture-war language and emotions, re-humanize a mob, and provide a generative path for its energy. Such a voice can call our tribes closer to an attitude of cultural stewardship.

The arts present the most powerful form of nonviolent resistance. Scout's actions in Harper Lee's creative lens—her willingness to step into a conflict and take a personal risk in order to call out *for both sides* their deepest humanity, highest ideals, and deepest longings—anticipated thousands of peaceful marches to come.[16]

Culture Care affirms this language of empathy, which is a fruit of love toward the "other."

---

16 Scout also reminds us of the difficulty of true nonviolence when she kicks a man in the shin for trying to remove Jem from the scene.

We need to create cultural contexts where this love toward the other, toward those outside our tribe's borders, is cultivated and modeled organically. A Culture Care environment will nourish and steward our abilities to dream even in the face of injustice, intolerance, and persecution.

Jesus told his followers, "I am sending you out like sheep among wolves. Therefore be as shrewd as snakes and as innocent as doves" (Matthew 10:16, NIV). Poets, artists, and creative catalysts can, like Scout, remain determinedly "innocent as doves" while being "wise as serpents" in using their creativity. Reminders of beauty can present justice in words, images, and songs that draw us in and captivate our attention until their truth can reach our hearts and transform our communities. Culture Care is the logical extension of nonviolent resistance to injustice.

In August 1963, prior to giving his "I Have a Dream" speech at the March on Washington, the Rev. Dr. Martin Luther King, Jr. found himself exhausted by a series of setbacks, imprisonments, oppressions, and disappointments. He was so physically spent that he spent many hours simply resting while his followers wrote the speech he was to give to the historic gathering. One of his close aides, Clarence Benjamin Jones, said that "the logistical preparations for the March were so burdensome that the speech was not a priority for us," and that, "on the evening of Tuesday, August 27, [twelve hours before the March] Martin still didn't know what he was going to say." After walking a few miles to the Lincoln Memorial, he stood to read the prepared text, but he knew something was not right.

Mahalia Jackson, the great Gospel singer who sang before he spoke, stood behind Dr. King throughout the prepared speech. As he read the text, she kept on yelling, "tell 'em about the dream, Martin; tell 'em about the dream!"

At the end of the prepared speech, Dr. King put down his text and began to speak extemporaneously; the energy of the crowd listening empowered him, and the result was the "I Have a Dream" we know today.

Imagine that—an artist pushing a tired preacher to preach from his heart. Dr. King was an artist of the dream, but it took another artist to recognize the artistry that was being held back by the context of the gathering.

Artists need to stand behind the podiums of preachers, teachers, and leaders and remind them to "tell 'em about the Dream!" Part of our calling is to remind leaders of what they are marching toward to begin with, to reach into the deepest recesses of *their own* visions. Sometimes, we may need to remind them to put down their prepared text. Artists who operate as *mearcstapas* can exhort in this way, in and out of a prepared tribal language into a visionary, extemporaneous "jazz" language of the heart. That music invites all to become extemporaneous artists of care.

One cold, rainy evening in New York City in 2010, I was invited to serve on a panel for a special screening of *Countdown to Zero,* a film about nuclear disarmament. The friend who organized the meeting was disappointed by the turnout; only about thirty people came. He apologized to the crowd, and to the panel, which also included civil rights leader Jesse Jackson, for the low turnout. Jackson stopped him: "I remember that day when Martin gave his famous sermon at the Riverside Church," Jackson said. "There were only about thirty people then, too."

The panel went on to discuss an initiative by President Ronald Reagan and President Mikhail Gorbachev to eliminate nuclear weapons. At one point, Jackson spoke up again. "It was only when Marvin Gaye started to sing that song ["What's Going On"] that our civil rights movement became a true movement." He looked me straight in the eye: "We need artists because they give us songs to sing to."

Connecting justice with beauty is essential. Any cause we believe in needs a song that everyone can sing, a song to march to or rally around, a song that will draw people in so they can learn to care. Artists are the ones to provide the music. But artists are not present just to entertain the crowd; like Mahalia Jackson, they can play a role to reveal the heart of a movement. This is possible because they, as *mearcstapas*, must learn not only to speak tribal languages, but also trade languages and creoles that connect people across boundaries. Artists are, in this sense, uniquely prepared to create beauty that is universal or points to the universal. They write songs that everyone can sing.

Artists are themselves leaders: they may never inspire with a speech, preach from a pulpit, or own a company, but they are leaders by the sheer fact of their awareness and observation, for the stories they tell and the language and symbols they create. Psychologist Howard Gardner, creator of the "multiple intelligences" theory, writes:

> *Indeed, creators and leaders are remarkably similar. Both groups seek to influence the thoughts and behaviors of other people. Both are, accordingly, engaged in the enterprise of persuasion. Moreover, each leader or creator has a story to tell: A creator is contributing to the story of a chosen domain; a leader is creating a story about his group. Finally, embodiment is important for both groups: A leader must embody her stories in her daily life; a creator must embody his story by carrying out work in his domain. The difference lies in the directness of this influence.*[17]

Mahalia Jackson's prompting of Dr. King released him to speak from the heart. But her own powerful artistic work, like Marvin Gaye's later, was even more so an "enterprise of persuasion," an effort, as she said, to "break down some of the hate and fear that divide" people. It was the work of a border-stalker. She used her indirect influence as

17 Howard E. Gardner, *Intelligence Reframed: Multiple Intelligences for the 21st Century.* Perseus
  Books, 2000, p. 130.

a creator to become a more direct leader. And she did so by staying true to her core convictions.

Not all artists can or should follow Jackson into overt leadership, but she is still someone all of us should emulate. Influence of any kind imposes responsibility, and Jackson is a model for influence that is well-invested. Artists have a responsibility to use their persuasive influence to create the "world that ought to be" and to avoid the misuse of their abilities that can become so self-destructive. One sure way do so is by using their influence to illuminate the path of empathy.

Two Lives
at the Margins

Artists as *mearcstapas* can provide significant cultural language or even new operative principles for our societies and churches. Harper Lee and Mahalia Jackson saw beyond their current realities. So too in their own times and places did the poet Emily Dickinson (1830–1886) and the painter Vincent van Gogh (1853–1890).

Emily and Vincent are concrete examples of *mearcstapas* living in times that prefigure ours. They anticipated the full flowering of modernity, intuiting the rise of utilitarian pragmatism and creating works that spoke—and are still speaking today—against dehumanization. Neither of them fit well with their culture. Both longed for their gifts to be acknowledged and cared for, but they left behind abundant evidence in their letters that this incompatibility arose from greater purposes, not always articulable, to which they felt called.

Both Emily and Vincent struggled in particular to fit into the context of their churches. I like to use their examples to point out some future possibilities of artists' roles in society and in the church. Their vision was creative and artistic, but it was also theological and intimately connected with what they considered to be true worship.

In the dashes

I see in their works a pilgrimage toward the margins of society, often intentionally moving away from their own secure borders of familial tribal culture. Vincent began to learn to draw when he, as an evangelist, spent time in the Belgian coal mines, sharing in the miserable darkness of the miners. Emily withdrew into a corner of her small room, yet in doing so she took flight in her poems.[18] Notice this 1879 poem on a hummingbird:[19]

> *A Route of Evanescence*
> *With a revolving Wheel —*
> *A Resonance of Emerald*
> *A Rush of Cochineal —*
> *And every Blossom on the Bush*
> *Adjusts its tumbled Head —*
> *The Mail from Tunis — probably,*
> *An easy Morning's Ride —*

This playful poem is an illumination. The mention of emerald and cochineal—burgundy dye extracted from a little Indian beetle, a dye that I use in my work—reinforces the pictorial quality of her poem. Her mention of Tunis, a North African city once known for piracy, connotes exotic adventure within a place where splendors of the past are hidden and revealed. Because she spent her life in Amherst, Massachusetts, Tunis serves more as a mental than physical location. Her references to foreign cities are comparable to van Gogh's perceptions of "Japan"—a foreign place of paradise inaccessible to the artist. The "route of evanescence" of a hummingbird lends such exotic splendor to a mail carrier's ordinary "morning ride."

This is a good example of how the very structure of her writing echoes what she observed in nature—the iambic rhythm of these verses, the slant rhymes (wheel/cochineal, head/ride) alternating between verses, and the alliterations (resonance/rush, tumbled/Tunis) weaving in and out, just like a hummingbird seeking nectar.

An artist's *mearcstapa* journey may not be a physical journey. In her poetry, identifying herself with a hummingbird, Emily is moving toward the margins. From her small window, she takes us on an imaginative border-stalking journey. The news of that far land

---

18 This section includes material adapted from "Refractions #36: 'The Hyphen of the Sea—A Journey with Emily Dickinson (Part 1)" (makotofujimura.com).

19 *The Poems of Emily Dickinson: Reading Edition*, edited by Ralph W. Franklin, Cambridge, Mass.: The Belknap Press of Harvard University Press, Copyright © 1951, 1955, 1979, 1983, 1998, 1999 by the President and Fellows of Harvard College.

("mail from Tunis") is both enticing and ominous. The "revolving wheel" reminds us of Ezekiel's vision,[20] and as in all her poems, she draws from a language learned as a daughter of Amherst Calvinists. Her rhythms are taken from hymns she has learned to play on the piano. It is also evident that her poems are confessions of how she deemed herself unfit for the church and chose not to participate even as the Great Awakening expanded in the north, and of her deep mourning for the costly sacrifice of the Civil War.

When I visited Emily Dickinson's Amherst home, our group was taken to her room on the second floor. There, along with a small bed, is a replica of her desk, the delicate, single-drawer wooden writing table she used to write her poems. It is made of cherry wood, seventeen and a half inches square.

One reminder from Emily's life is that one needs nothing more than a small and dedicated space to make a significant impact in culture. She had neither publisher nor an encouraging writing environment— no one even knew she was writing so much poetry. But she had her desk, and a lamp by which to wake up, every day at three in the morning, to write.

In order to be generative, we may have to find ways to protect our creativity in light of limited resources. When I speak to artists' groups, I often ask, "do you have your own 'seventeen-and-a-half-inch' desk dedicated to your craft?"

Emily's well-documented struggles with faith place her at the edge of faith and cultural discourse; yet it is precisely because of her struggles that she is valuable to the church and anyone who desires to wrestle deeply with faith, art, and culture.

---

20 See the book of Ezekiel, especially chapters 1, 3, 10, and 11.

I have found as a local leader in communities and churches that others do not know what to do with you if you identify yourself as an artist. Things go much more smoothly if you are a lawyer or accountant. In church and parachurch ministry leadership training, those who do not "fit into" the agenda of preset programs are often marked as hard to disciple, or even as unfaithful.

Emily Dickinson, as a young girl attending a prestigious school in Amherst, experienced something similar, though more pointed.[21] Her schoolmaster, Mary Lyons, was the founder of Mount Holyoke Female Seminary—and an evangelist. Lyons created categories for young girls, and regularly divided her students into three public groups: Committed followers of Christ ("Christians"); those hoping to become Christians ("Hopers"); and those who were without hope to become Christians ("No-Hopers"). Lyons placed Emily in the third category.[22]

Emily refused to participate in the waves of revivalism that swept Amherst and in which family members and friends experienced conversion. She wrote to her friend Jane Humphrey: "Christ is calling everyone here, all my companions have answered, even my darling Vinnie believes she loves, and trusts him, and I am standing alone in rebellion."

Maintaining her integrity alone surely took a measure of courage. That "rebellion" may have been awakened early by the sudden death of Emily's thirteen-year-old friend Sophia Holland, an event that affected her so deeply that she fell ill and had to take time off from school. She was then an exceptionally private but articulate young girl, whose early childhood letters demonstrate her enthusiasm for learning and writing through witty and verbose run-on sentences. Reading her life's letters is an ongoing encounter with death. One sees the run-on sentences replaced by multiple dashes. These dashes remained her unique expression and identity—she saw herself in the dashes, in the liminal, transitional space between life and death. In theory, each death could have been an opportunity to exercise the

---

21 Also adapted from "Refractions #36," (makotofujimura.com).
22 "Emily Dickinson at Mount Holyoke," Sydney R. McLean, *The New England Quarterly*, Vol. 7, No. 1 (March, 1934), pp. 25–42.

Puritan teaching of seeking the eternal, but Emily felt each loss so keenly that instead she came to deeply question God's goodness, and was drawn further into lament and isolation.

As she matured in her rejection of Calvinist theology, her satirical language sharpened. But her rebellion was as much against the rigid and imprecise categories by which people try to obscure the world's complexity and suffering. Such categories can become attempts to reduce the wheels of Ezekiel's vision, in all their beauty and terror, to the regulated gears of a grandfather clock. They are attempts to cage a hummingbird.

Into the Starry Night

Not much later but in another corner of the earth, Vincent van Gogh painted, haunted by the parallel specter of his own liminal existence. While Emily Dickinson chose to stay at home, Vincent journeyed far from his home in the Netherlands, first as an evangelist among the coal miners in Belgium, and ultimately to Arles, France, where he met his early death.

Not many know that Vincent was born into a line of Dutch Reformed pastors and that he himself trained for the pastorate. It was only when the church elders rejected his call that he turned to work as an evangelist. He lived among the poor with Franciscan devotion. But the authorities who sent him were appalled by the squalid conditions he chose to share. They rejected him again and pronounced him "unfit for the dignity of the priesthood."

The double rejection by the church of his desire to fully incarnate himself in the lives of coal miners must have been deeply painful. Little wonder that he, like Emily, came to reject "the God of the clergymen."[23] But he did not lose his awareness of God's presence in the lives of the poor, nor his sense of God urging him to love others. It was while toiling in the Belgian coal mines that he began to draw portraits of the miners. He was not at that point formally trained in painting or drawing and yet, as he drew, he discovered that visually

23 Letter (#164) from Vincent van Gogh to Theo van Gogh, c. 21 December 1881.

he could communicate more deeply about the compassion he felt for humanity than he could verbally in the pulpit. "I feel that there is nothing more truly artistic than to love people," he wrote.

Art became a way for him to capture, even by candlelight, the genesis moments hidden behind every darkened face—a way to tap into the potential of each moment, to see afresh life's struggles in the light of Christ's presence. His paintings are color-filled parables of genesis moments, generatively given to us in flesh with canvas and paint. By the time of his tragic death, he had only had three years of devoting his life to the paintings that he is known for, the works now in the collections of museums all over the world.

Time spent in consideration of his famous *Starry Night* can become a journey into the heart of a *mearcstapa*. The painting is set in Arles, France. Notice that at the very center of the painting is a white Dutch Reformed church. Vincent imported a church building from his childhood, pasting it into the French landscape to create a parable of his own life.

If you obscure the church by placing a finger over it, the painting falls apart visually. The church is the only vertical form, aside from the dominant cypress tree on the left, which juts out to break the horizontal planes. The tree and the church are the two forms that connect heaven and earth. Without the church, the cypress takes over the swirl of movement and there is no visual center to hold the painting in tension.[24]

Notice, too, how the homes surrounding the church are lit with warm light. The church is the only building in the painting that is completely dark. Herein lies Vincent's message, particular to the reality of being a border-stalker: the Spirit has left the church— at least the building—but is active in nature. If you follow the visual flow of the painting, your eye will cycle upward, still anchored

24 This section and portions of the following chapter are adapted from my 2012 commencement address to the graduate school at Biola University. The full text can be found at makotofujimura.com.

by the church building. Your gaze will come to rest in the upper right corner, on the Sun/Moon. This is not just a moon, nor a sun, but a combination. Vincent wanted to show that the Spirit of God transcends even nature—that in the Resurrection, in the New Earth and the New Heaven, a complete new order will shape the things to come.

On June 23, 1888, Vincent wrote to Emile Bernard, a younger artist:

> *(But seeing that nothing opposes it—) supposing that there are also lines and forms as well as colors on the other innumerable planets and suns—it would remain praiseworthy of us to maintain a certain serenity with regard to the possibilities of painting under superior and changed conditions of existence, an existence changed by a phenomenon no queerer and no more surprising than the transformation of the caterpillar into a butterfly, or of the white grub into a cockchafer.*

You and I are caterpillars about to be transformed into butterflies. We are on the threshold of seeing what the biblical scholar N. T. Wright calls the post-Resurrection reality of "life *after* 'life after death'."

Vincent painted this "superior and changed condition of existence" as already here—but not yet fully so. He developed a visual diction that serves as a bridge between our current condition and a future transformed, genesis condition. He envisioned the transformation and by faith painted the world to come, as a *mearcstapa* walking the borders between earth and heaven. He also depicted a world that he was intuiting, a world in which the church still holds things together structurally, but one in which the light has gone out of the church building.

Our Calling
in the Starry Night

Art poses questions. It probes into our lives as living parables. One question we need to face is: *What do we do if Vincent is right?* What do we do in a culture in which the light of the Spirit has departed church buildings and gone swirling instead into nature, into life's margins? What do we do in a culture in which the church is viewed as only a lifeless structural memory of the moral underpinnings that keep the world from falling apart?

For we are living in the world Vincent depicted. The church has kept the structure of truth, but we have largely lost touch with the Spirit in creating beauty. The church is no longer where the masses come to know the Creator of beauty. Tim Keller, my former pastor, says that Christians have invited in Jesus as our Savior, but we also need to invite him in as our Creator.

Many have noted that members of our emerging generations are not eager to join a church. The fastest growing denomination, I am told, is "none." These younger people show little interest in denominationalism, and yet it does not seem that they are done with Jesus or the life of the Spirit. They have far more investment in seeking justice and caring for our environment than did my generation. Perhaps many in the younger generations are becoming *mearcstapas*, artists of the borders and margins.

Useful or valuable?

In recent times, the arts have been seen as useful to the economy— but that surely misses the point of why we need to care for culture. Evaluating the arts based on an economic metric makes utility the bottom line, distorting our vision of the world that ought to be.

Utilitarian pragmatism is tied to a world in which vision is stripped of transcendence. Before the modern age in the West, the narrative of Christendom provided a vision of the world in which the "bottom line" was the full thriving of humanity. Lacking that vision, we have become accustomed to a reality where anything and anyone not valued at the moment can be disposable.

Sometimes we become aware of our own unconscious choice of utility and fragmentation over beauty and thriving by our reactions, just as my reaction to Judy's care revealed my assumptions. Often our initial intent is appropriate: pragmatic and responsible decision-making. Feeding ourselves over the coming weekend is good. But that is not our "chief end" (in the famous words of the Westminster Shorter Catechism). Our calling, simply as humans—and more so as followers of Christ—is wider than our career and our survival, even in the modern age.

Utilitarian thinking is often disguised, but it still can result in life-long entrapment if it is allowed in. Take the example of college. Most of us have been pragmatists, seeing college as a transactional entity in which the student spends four years of time and tuition to receive back a lucrative career. Parents advise their children to major in something "useful" rather than in the humanities, often under threat of withholding financial support. Desiring a sustainable career is noble, but such recommendations debase education—and our humanity. The pragmatic goal of having a "useful degree" can calcify into a dogma—or worse, reaffirm an unquestioned assumption—that you are only worthwhile if you are useful.

This is one of the effects of living in a culture where usefulness is the highest virtue. We are too prone to see a human being or human endeavor as worthwhile only as it is useful to the whole, whether that be a company, family, community, or even a church. The corollary is that individuals who do not meet this standard are "other," an attitude that results effectively in their exile from the functioning, "normal" world. Those who are disabled, those who are oppressed or weakened, or those who are without a voice are soon implicitly regarded as useless, and then as disposable.

Little wonder that some groups are pushing to grant our elderly and disabled people the "right to die," and that many are willing to be persuaded by arguments like those being made by philosopher Peter Singer and atheist evangelist Richard Dawkins for the elimination of Down Syndrome children. Suffice it to say that such arguments are logical only granting the dogma of our being trapped with limited resources in a materialist world where those who are considered useless take up resources "needed" for normal human beings. Too often, belief in such a world calls into being a utilitarian machinery of homogeneity, manipulation, and control run by those who presume to speak for the human species or the environment. But many of us, or perhaps all of us, will be deemed "useless" at some level in such a model.

Called beyond utility

Culture Care values reach far beyond materialism to the ultimate human value of love—toward a generative reality. Artists know instinctively that beauty, delight, and wonderment lie beyond the resources we assume we have, so they are often the whistle-blowers who bring constricted and distorted visions to our attention. Their intuitions give birth to music, art, dance, and poetry that defiantly and joyfully reach beyond the closed boundaries of nature into the mystery of existence. Artistic expressions are signposts declaring what it is to be fully human.

Art is ultimately not "useful." It serves no practical function. This is why it is indispensable, especially in the modern age. Dana Gioia has rightly said that we "do not provide arts education to create more artists, though that is a byproduct. The real purpose of arts education is to create complete human beings capable of leading successful and productive lives in a free society."[25] We provide arts education so that we can have better teachers, doctors, engineers, mothers, and fathers. Arts are not a luxury but a path to educate the whole individual toward thriving. They are needed simply because a civilization cannot be a civilization without the arts. A great civilization is an art form of the highest order.

25 Dana Gioia, Commencement address at Stanford University, Stanford, California, June 18, 2007.

Business, education, and even the arts "industry" are driven (sometimes unawares) by utilitarian thinking. Even in defining "calling" today, we often succumb to pragmatism. I have often heard church leaders say that if you do not have an opportunity to find an audience for your gifts, this is a sign that you are not "called" to that field of endeavor. Respond to the "needs" of the world, they advise. Had Emily and Vincent followed such pragmatic advice, we would not have their art today. Neither found an audience for their art in their lifetime, but they were indeed called to their art, and there is much to learn from their journeys—not least because of their unfulfilled promise.

Mearcstapas are *called* into the margins, into stalking the borders, moving between traditional tribes and the unknown. Vincent and Emily created in response to their own internal compasses, their own *urgency of need to create.* They both followed, quite consciously, the ultimate master *mearcstapa,* Jesus. They simply could not follow any other path.

Artists are often mislabeled as impractical because their intuition senses cultural realities before these are manifested in society. And certainly Emily and Vincent saw the true needs of their culture. They were guided by the Spirit, who spoke into their art and showed them the fractured tribal realities of our emerging modern time, to which they responded by speaking a prophetic language of reconciliation.

In their lifetimes, Emily and Vincent were forced to operate in predetermined categories, strictly limited domains of how they were to serve God. Such categories, while often created with the best of intentions, are reductionist. They limit how we view humanity, not to mention God, and do not take into account the deep wrestling with faith, or its lack, that is so often part of the *mearcstapa* journey. Artists often confound pragmatic labels and bristle against the inbuilt dehumanization and fragmentation of categories. In that sense, all artists are *mearcstapas,* guiding us toward a world of abundance and complexity.

Younger artists often ask me whether their art is "good enough," and whether they are called to be an artist. My answer is: "if you are not sure, you are not called." That may seem harsh, but the reality of the arts requires that we follow our calling no matter what others think, or even what we believe ourselves. When art is simply what we must do to stay true to ourselves, it is a calling.

It is not surprising that Emily and Vincent—and their art—were marginalized, for both intuited that such an exiled existence was the only way to remain consistent with their humanity given the cultural pressures of their time. Yet more than a century later these two exiled souls still speak eloquently to what our hearts long for. Her poems give us words to express our own resistance to utility. His paintings offer parables of beauty that sow seeds of authentic being into our wounded, dehumanized souls. Their works are antidotes to the utilitarian drive for commercial and ideological gain, remedies for the poison in the river of culture. They offer our dying culture unfading bouquets, gifts of enduring beauty that we do not want to refuse.

Every challenge is an opportunity to exercise generative thinking, to think through the fears and seek out the light that still shines, however obscured. The psalmist tells us that "the heavens declare the glory of God" (Psalm 19). If the church is darkened, perhaps we should focus on where the Spirit is moving and pay attention to where the colors are the most intense. The Gospel reality speaks not just of what we do inside our churches, but of the presence of the divine already evident in nature and in all human creativity.

In a world in which churches are seen as darkened, we cannot practice "Sunday" faith and live as if Christ is not present in the rest of the week. We need to acknowledge the presence of grace in the darkest of areas, even—especially—in the areas we would rather hide from God. Instead of speaking of God primarily in personal life and church settings, we must proclaim God as the source of all illuminating life. We must find God in the very fabric of our callings as teachers, as nurses, as engineers, as artists, and as writers. We must see our occupations as part of the glorious reality in which God has already manifested the Spirit's incorruptible visage.

The church is not a building, but the collective souls of the people whom God is calling to deep life and eternal fellowship with himself. Whether we are politicians, dancers, entrepreneurs, or plumbers, we are called into the Starry Night of our complex existence, as we, too, swirl into the darker mystery of our twenty-first century vista. Because the "heavens declare the glory of God" we must be fragrant torches of truth and justice, carrying the aroma of beauty outside of the walls of our institutions. We can also bring our small offerings as lighted candles back to darkened church sanctuaries. The darker the building, the more pronounced such small acts of service will seem.

We can follow Christ's call, creating in love, as Vincent did—loving the world that rejected him and longing to be at home in the church, the only building without light. Christ, the Light of the world, is the ultimate *mearcstapa*, a shepherd-artist, border-stalking our tribal existence, and bringing the light of the Good News from the New Tribe that is already here and yet to come. Christ's light will shine through every darkness and will not be extinguished.

Western Christianity in the twentieth century fell into an "adjective" existence with Christian music, Christian art, Christian plumbers. Even today, artists are often valued *in* the church only if they create art *for* the church, or at least "Christian art." Culture Care will mean moving away from such labels. There is no need to disown these terms absolutely, but we do need to realize that these categories in themselves are concessions to modernist pressures. They are a voluntary surrender to utilitarian pragmatism, and their use leads only to disdain and indifference. Ultimately, these terms undermine our mandate to infuse all of life with Christ's presence.

I am not a Christian artist. I am a Christian, yes, and an artist. I dare not treat the powerful presence of Christ in my life as an adjective.

I want Christ to be my whole being. Vincent van Gogh was not a Christian artist either, but in Christ he painted the heavens declaring the glory of God. Emily Dickinson was not a Christian artist, and yet through her honest wrestling, given wings in words, her works—like Vincent's, like Harper Lee's, like Mahalia Jackson's—speak to all the world as integrated visions of beauty against injustice.

It is time for followers of Christ to let Christ be the noun in our lives, to let our whole being ooze out like a painter's colors with the splendor and the mystery of Christ, the inexhaustible beauty that draws people in. It is time to follow the Spirit into the margins and outside the doors of the church.

Opening the Gates

What kind of a framework is needed to guide *mearcstapas*—to prepare them for success on their mission?

Recently, an artist friend noted that in John 10, the parable of the shepherd and his sheep, Jesus speaks of a reality in which the gate is opened into the world, and "I am the gate for the sheep" (John 10:7, NIV). The open gate is why a sheep may leave the flock and be lost (as in Luke 15). The shepherd's job is to guide sheep through the gate and beyond, to help them find the best grass, and to protect them—not to keep them shut in their pen. The pen has a clear function, but we do not need a "good shepherd" if the sheep are always locked up, "safe" from harm.

Jesus, however, promises safety both inside and outside the sheepfold: "I am the Gate. Anyone who goes through me will be cared for—will freely go in and out, and find pasture" (John 10:9, The Message). The word here translated "cared for" ("saved" in many translations) means to preserve something safe and unharmed, to keep something from being lost, and also to cure, heal, or restore to full health. The sheep in this image are made safe explicitly for the purpose of going out and coming in—to cross borders, we might say—so they can thrive.

In recent years, many churches and communities have missed this point. We have created rigid tribal boundaries with high barriers and closed gates to keep our sheep in the pen, safe from the wider world. Ironically, closed gates mandate the extra labor and expense of bringing in stale, dry fodder—everything "Christian" needed to feed the flock—for sheep who should be grazing green pastures for themselves.

This leaves our lively young sheep with a perceived choice between complying with a community's norms and starving culturally, or leaping the fence to get cultural nourishment. Our call as leaders and parents is instead to open the gate and guide them to the greater pastures.

Are we willing as a community or as churches to do that? Opening the gate will mean accepting a loss of control. It will mean exposing our children and our students to certain dangers. They will mix with other flocks, and sometimes we may have to go look for one that gets lost, and leave the "ninety-nine sheep behind" (Luke 15:4). We will confront variable weather, predatory presences, and our own limits as shepherds. But the Good Shepherd promises to journey with us. Will we rely on him to do as he says?

It is not just the border-stalkers, but all of us in the sheepfold who need to "go in and out" for our flourishing. If we can raise and train *mearcstapas* in their challenging role, this gifted group of folks may be able to learn to read the weather and inform us of dangers and opportunities, so that the whole flock will be better able to navigate the outer world of culture.

C.J.

Our second son, C.J., was just such a child.[26] I remember walking with him in the streets of New York City. Even as a young child he noticed things that I ignored, like the homeless folks or graffiti. He showed an early inclination to music and art, often bringing his skateboard to the edges of Manhattan and crossing into Brooklyn (well before Brooklyn was hip). He is a *mearcstapa*.

C.J. had, as he would readily admit, a very colorful teenage life. He struggled with his faith and his church commitments. During some dark days in his teens he violated many boundaries, and I feared at one point I had lost him as a son. These days were some of the most challenging of my life as a parent, but I also now

---

26 I am grateful for the journey that C.J. has led to teach me of the *mearcstapa* role. This chapter is a gift from him to the reader, with his permission.

recall them, as I write this, as some of the most rewarding. Even though C.J. has now "come home" in many ways, he still wrestles deeply with issues of faith and art. Today, a college graduate with degrees in music composition and philosophy, he is producing and writing his "collage" music and helping his girlfriend develop her theatre company.

When he was about twelve, C.J. became interested in what would become hip-hop music. When he came to me with his interest, Judy and I decided to "train a child in the path he should go" (meaning not "the way *we* think he should go"). I knew very little about that musical world, but we told him that he was welcome to listen to any song as long as he shared it with us and we could discuss it. (We did not give this permission to either his older brother or younger sister, although they, too, would grow into creative human beings. It was something only C.J. was allowed to do early.) I also arranged for a friend who was studying for a PhD in composition from Columbia University to come every Saturday and teach him music theory.

I asked a pastor friend in the Newark slums if he could recommend any up-and-coming musicians. One of these was Kanye West, then an unknown from Chicago. I began to listen to West, then Eminem, Lauryn Hill, and Outkast. I never expected to be listening to "explicit" versions of many of their songs on my computer; I often struggled with hip-hop and the lifestyle and language choices of which the art form spoke. C.J. warned me of these things even as a young person, noting too that "non-explicit" versions lack the power and eloquence of the originals. I have come to realize that he was right.

As a *mearcstapa*, C.J. guided me into the world of hip-hop, and continues to do so. When he went to college, he and his girlfriend realized that the university culture offered only two options: library culture—to get straight As, or frat culture—to drink and relieve stress. There was no alternative. So C.J. began to experiment with a Friday evening gathering called "Bankwet" (spelled differently each time), with hip-hop/rap performances, poetry readings, and art. He mentored many creative types, leading them to develop their craft. His girlfriend, Tina, a straight-A theatre student, opted out of the stage production role she could have had in order to make her senior thesis a guerrilla theatre project that exposed what university students were truly thinking and struggling with.

When Judy and I arrived for his graduation, they spontaneously gathered all the folks involved in the Bankwet group. They performed for us and together we celebrated their time at the university. What I noticed, to my delight, was that this group of creatives was the most diverse (culturally and racially) of any I have known at this university. C.J. and Tina instinctively brought together all its "tribes."

It would not be true to say that every decision our children have made aligns with my faith and values; but a reality of dealing with border-stalkers is that often they do not toe the line of conventionality. But as they hold to deeper values, they have the capacity to show us the possibilities, the green pastures, which exist beyond our tribal norms.

'I have other sheep'[27]

The visible church is the sheepfold. For too long, we have held the gate shut and our members, especially children like C.J., have been starving culturally because we have lacked a proper guiding theology to explore and graze the cultural fields. We need to be reminded regularly that the Holy Spirit is active well beyond our walls that God continually blesses all human beings, regardless of where they are in relationship with him.

Just as an ecosystem necessitates complexity and dependency of interaction, visible and invisible, so with the culture at large: God provides for us both inside and outside the visible church. In the lavishness—the gratuitousness—of God's common grace, the Holy Spirit is active in the wider culture as well, making green the grass outside the fold. Through the Holy Spirit's guidance, and his filling

27 This section is adapted from material originally published in: "Artist in Residence Series: Culture Care for Churches," March 26, 2014 at *Transpositions*, the blog of the Institute for Theology, Imagination, and the Arts at the University of St Andrews (transpositions.co.uk).

of our lives with God's love, the Good Shepherd can guide us into the best pastures in the furthest reaches of culture.

In Matthew 5:45, Jesus tells us that God "makes his sun rise on the evil and on the good, and sends rain on the just and on the unjust." This passage is often used by Christians to ground a theological understanding of common grace, but many discussions of this topic miss the connection with what Jesus says immediately before this:

> *"You have heard that it was said, 'You shall love your neighbor and hate your enemy.' But I say to you, Love your enemies and pray for those who persecute you, so that you may be sons of your Father who is in heaven"* (Matthew 5:43–45a, NIV).

If we are to follow Jesus, we must practice living in the light of common grace, and we must therefore learn practically how to love our enemies. This love begins in recognition that our enemies have the ability to become a part of God's church, his flock, as God's Spirit reconciles them to himself. Even those who are currently God's enemies are people we need to treat as creatures God made and God loves. These enemies, these "others" are among Jesus' "other sheep," those "not of this sheep pen," the sheep he promises to bring in (John 10:16, NIV).

The Holy Spirit is active at the margins of our churches, drawing people in. When we hold our gate shut, we not only starve our own sheep, our pursuit of "safety" becomes a barrier to entry for Jesus' other sheep.

As I've developed this thesis, I have come to realize that at the heart of Culture Care is my desire to know the full depth of the Gospel of Jesus Christ. What is the "Good News"? The reductionism of our modern assumptions has caused the Gospel to be truncated, limited to pragmatic and tribal concerns rather than the Good News of the whole of the Bible—true life, the never-ending restoration of all things in Christ.

Culture Care emphasizes that God cares for the *whole* of the creation (as his own artwork) and for history (as God's own story lived through our fallen reality), and that there is not one hair of our head or one moment of our journey that God does not pay close attention to (Luke 12:7). Culture Care takes Jesus himself, who cared for people, his surroundings, and his culture, as a model for us all.

Even though Culture Care, as a term, grows out of Creation Care and Soul Care, my intended audience is wider than the Christian community. I want to speak also to those who long for beauty, to those who may not yet have recognized the need for an outward expression of Christ in their lives.

My initial reason for coming up with generative language is to translate the "Spirit-filled life" into terms that people outside the visible church can understand and resonate with. Even many artists who despise the church (I can name them, as they are my friends) love to speak of, or about, Jesus. I try to find a common language to speak to them about the Spirit's operation. When I do, they often recognize the Spirit, without naming him, in their studios, rehearsal halls, and poems. These observations by outsiders are critical for my understanding of culture at large; they are the grass outside of the sheepfold that feeds this sheep.

We need open gates. But we need the sheepfold too. Even for a *mearcstapa* who is skilled at living in the wider world, the welcome and safety of a sheepfold cannot be overstated. Border-stalkers need a solid grounding, a secure place to which they can return: a parabola requires a center to spin out of. The further and more powerful the parabolic movement, the stronger the center needs to be.[28]

A healthy community is one that is secure, anchored in tradition and faith, but also allowing for a dynamic movement outward, sending forth artists and missionaries, caregivers and entrepreneurs. It is centered and confident in its identity as a flock because it knows the

28 Thanks to Gordon Pennington for this observation.

purpose for which the Good Shepherd has gathered it: to serve and bless and transform the wider world.

Where are such healthy communities? Do any exist today? Part of our future Culture Care journey will be to identify communities and groups that are working to cultivate these values. We may see glimpses of the potential of what a community "ought to be," but I am sure all communities suffer from lack of grace or in lack of care for those in the margins. We may need to begin, therefore, by considering the cultural soil conditions; by a careful analysis, we may come up with strategies to strengthen what is healthy and compensate for factors that may compromise our vitality.

Cultivating Cultural Soil

I recently moved out of the city, and I have been gardening. I am a novice gardener, but I have realized that what I do as an artist—as a practitioner of the ancient art of Nihonga, the slow rhythm of creating a new work layer by layer over a period of time—is very similar to cultivating the right soil for my garden.

Holding soil in your hands can lead to deeper meditations on Culture Care.

Soil is a complex reality. Most of us do not give a thought to the fact that soil is made of decomposed dead animals, plants, and insects. I plant my seeds in what is essentially a layered mass of death, accumulated over time. Good soil also contains other things we desire as gardeners—microorganisms, worms, and nutrients that make an environment conducive for seeds to come alive.

Apply this knowledge to culture at large. Culture, too, is full of "dead" objects from the past. A museum is a container for such detritus, though a good museum will make it come to life in contemporary context. Today's shifting market in art and commerce is leaving behind even more layers of cultural death. The difference is that, instead of past objects being reanimated in a museum, millions of cultural products now remain dormant or dead in cyberspace and in artists' studios.

If we assume, though, that winter is necessary for the spring—that death is essential for life to emerge—then our bleak and painful period is perhaps a necessary step toward the cultivation of a renewed culture. As the poet Christian Wiman puts it, "We live in and by our senses, which are conditioned in and by our deaths."[29] Cultivating—plowing, tilling—the cultural soil will loosen and aerate the various strata of earlier cultural products and ideas, making their nourishment available to new seeds and leaving our soil ready for the long-awaited thaw. When the "seeds" of art (and our lives) are planted in it, and the spring rains come, a culture can come alive again.

Cultural soil and the Gospel

Good soil is essential for a garden. As Jesus teaches in the parable of the sower and the soils in Matthew 13, no matter how good a seed is (and Jesus' seeds are the Gospel, perfectly pristine and good), it cannot produce fruit in soil that does not allow for deep roots.

What Christians call the Gospel—the "Good News"—includes a narrative of God's work from beginning to eternity that is often summarized as creation, fall, redemption, and restoration. It begins with God's good, beautiful, and gratuitous creation (and with humankind called very good). Humans broke away from God's purposes in Eden, and our rebellion results in ongoing fragmentation, separation, decay, and death. To redeem from death the creatures he still loves, God has acted in human history through Israel—and has come to us himself in Jesus, Israel's Messiah. When Christ returns again as he has promised, we will see the full renewal of creation and the restoration of all things.

What is more, if the Christians are correct, the death-defeating power of Christ is active now. It operates through God's Spirit enlivening his followers. The deep life of heaven is renewing the earth. We are even now, in part, beginning to see God's will done on earth. We live now in the era in which God has invited us—more accurately, has commanded us—to participate in his creative purposes, to extend his artistry, and to contribute to the restoration of all kinds of disorder. When Jesus speaks of the "seed," he is speaking toward this reintegration, the new reality breaking into our

29 Christian Wiman, "Varieties of Quiet," *Image 73*, 2012.

brokenness through the Spirit. It is characteristic of God's work that restoration grows from the smallest and most unlikely beginnings.

I see God as the ultimate Artist and we, still bearing God's image even in our fall, as artists writ small. The Bible is a book written by the creator God, spoken through God's creative if sometimes broken people. It is designed to recalibrate our worldview and reconnect us with God. Only then can God's power work through us as we fill—creatively and lovingly—the roles that contribute to God's work of restoration, which is a part of the purpose for which we were made and by which we thrive.

Our current culture, often called a "culture of death," is full of pointers toward the first two of these elements (creation and fall), but only rarely reflects, even in the churches, the full story of God's love and his ongoing work toward our full thriving. I have noticed, as an artist prone to looking on from the margins, that churches often present the middle two (fall and redemption), but rarely connect the whole story of the Bible—or the deep and restorative life now active in the world—with the stories of our present lives and communities. We often misuse this great book, reducing it to a book of rules, a checklist for earning our way into heaven, or a guidebook for material prosperity or personal well-being. Many churches replace God as Artist with God as "CEO of the universe" and turn to business metrics to measure their "success" at meeting his "bottom lines."

Christian communities are thus often busy with programs but rarely seen as a creative force to be reckoned with, let alone as a power of good that affects whole cities and gives everyone a song to sing. But as we, more and more, become gatherings of diverse people journeying together, as we learn truly to love each other with all our differences, we may help prepare the conditions in which God's good seed may bring forth new cultural life.

I see in the parable of the soils a call to a specific kind of cultural work. The new life the seed carries is beyond our capacity to provide. But we can and must contribute to the soil in which it will grow, and our efforts can affect the seed's fruitfulness. Culture Care thus prepares the way for the Gospel to spread.

The tilling of the soil is the most important task we can do to prepare ourselves and our culture for the seeds of the Gospel that God sows so lavishly. Beauty can sometimes break through our bedrock assumptions and prepare us to consider possibilities beyond the broken wasteland of our world, just as Judy's bouquet exposed my inner pragmatism, my "wasteland" vision, and started my journey toward faith and thriving. Then there are the thorns—"the worries of this life and the deceitfulness of wealth"—that Jesus warns us will compete with the good seed and make it unfruitful (Matthew 13:22). Art and other Culture Care work can sometimes thin out such weeds, releasing the full generative potential of God's seed.

Soil to thrive in

The God revealed in the Bible has endowed a Creation overflowing with beauty. This God is not characterized by utility but by abundant love. God desires his creatures—especially those who, in Christ, are adopted as his children—also to be creative and generative.

As we begin as Culture Care gardeners, we may need to learn to think beyond our immediate context. A person who owns a backyard pond is able on one level to make decisions about her pond without consciously considering larger ecological issues. Her concern is that the pond be free of mosquitoes, but a greater scope of awareness is crucial. Morally, she is responsible to learn the effects on the wider ecosystem of a pesticide that kills mosquitoes. The same process of widening our sphere of concern and anticipating the consequences or ripple effects of our actions also applies to culture.

We will not agree on every definition or approach. A dandelion is a weed to some, while to others it's part of their salad. But what is critical for our mindset is the *care* of culture. When we care for and love a parcel of land, we approach it very differently than if we simply consider it as a transactional commodity. Even if two neighbors don't see eye to eye on the use of their fields, if each truly cares for their land, they can pursue the same larger goal—to leave the land for their children and grandchildren to enjoy. We can do the same as we tend our culture, albeit in slightly different ways.

Wendell Berry, a true prophet of our time, wrote a reflection on the land promised to Abraham and his descendants, the people of Israel, for a magazine devoted to Creation Care. But it is applicable as much to cultural soils as to a farmer's soil:

> *The difficulty but also the wonder of the story of the Promised Land is that, there, the primordial and still continuing dark story of human rapaciousness begins to be accompanied by a vein of light which, however improbably and uncertainly, still accompanies us. This light originates in the idea of the land as a gift—not a free or a deserved gift, but a gift given upon certain rigorous conditions.*[30]

Notice some of the elements revealed on the path over which Berry skillfully guides us toward wise stewardship. First, as we journey toward Culture Care we must recognize that we will face the "dark story of human rapaciousness." We may encounter those who value in culture only the potential for gain. We may encounter apathy and even hostility if we care about the future. But lest cynicism take over, we make our journey, as Berry points out, alongside "a vein of light." Another way to say this is that the gift given to us as makers of culture is in its nature generative. The "rigorous conditions" include our active work in tilling the soil. If the soil conditions are right, we will find our thriving.

I began my journey as an artist very early on, responding to the realization that I am built to see things differently, to question deeply the nature of reality. But today I do much more than painting. I began the efforts of International Arts Movement, and now I am embarking on the core educational element of IAM, the Fujimura Institute. I have done so because, as I developed as an artist and as my career grew, I came to another realization: The soil of the culture in which I was planted was not soil I could thrive in. The gift of art is not allowed to grow in our highly commoditized system.

In a remarkably prescient book, *The Gift*, poet Lewis Hyde, helps to explain the problem. He writes in the introduction:

> *It is the assumption of this book that a work of art is a gift, not a commodity. Or, to state the modern case with more precision, that works of art exist simultaneously in two "economies," a market economy and a gift economy. Only one of these is essential however: a work of art can survive without the market, but where there is no gift, there is no art.*[31]

Let me borrow an analogy that Hyde uses. Before Western people came to the Pacific Northwest, Native Americans managed the salmon. They accepted salmon as a gift. They took what was necessary and trusted each year that more would come. When Westerners came and applied early modern methods to the fisheries, salmon became commodities—and the salmon population plummeted until people realized that the species must be protected from unrestrained commercial forces.

The same principle applies to the arts. The ideal conditions for the arts include a communal recognition that they are a gift to society and need some protection. The arts are a unique exception to the capitalist argument. There is nothing wrong with artists marketing their art, or patrons purchasing art, but we must recognize that the arts belong primarily in the precinct of a gift economy and that artists who swim in the waters of culture need to be protected from market forces if their cultural contributions—or sometimes they themselves—are to survive.

We have seen in recent decades how care for the natural environment, like the Hudson River, has led to great renewal. Nature has its own generative power, and human stewardship can be multiplied by nature's own power to restore herself. Culture, I

---

31 Lewis Hyde, *The Gift*, 1983. Second Vintage Books edition, 2007, p. xvi.

believe, has an even greater power to restore because human gifting is already generative by nature. The human creative gift can also be powerfully healing and generative, reconciling the greatest of enemies, bridging the greatest of gaps.

It's not enough to have artists who seek after beauty, truth, and goodness; we must have churches, policies, and communities that reflect a long-term nurture of culture that is beautiful, truthful, and full of goodness.

Through Culture Care, we need to initiate a series of models— cultural greenhouses or gardens, contained environments that allow artists to work in conditions where they can thrive, where art's "gift" function is recognized and valued. We need the right type of protected arenas with good gardeners to till the soil.

As I have thought about such creative microcosms, I have come to see that the image of a greenhouse is not strong enough for what is needed. Greenhouses imply a strongly sheltered environment where soil and plants are protected from the weather. They are also resource-intensive, requiring careful monitoring for humidity, temperature, and other factors. And their produce, while visually appealing, often lacks in taste when compared with crops raised in the open. The "garden" concept is better, open as it is to the wind and rain, yet gardens also are contained within walls, a planned space, and with a limited scope or audience. In trying to create ideal conditions for artists, both seem to fall into an emphasis on "protection" at the expense of "gift to the society."

Both of these models will be appropriate at times to allow new artists to take root in a dry or poisoned climate, or during a frigid season, but too much time in the greenhouse is counterproductive to work that is sustainable and generative. I suspect that implementing a garden or greenhouse environment for artists is more likely to result in "Christian art" than "art from Christians." And one can already predict how unappealing such spaces would be to restless young *mearcstapas*, already primed to jump the fence.

Where is nature's most generative place? Is there a natural habitat we can emulate for artists and culture shapers that combines a reasonable amount of protection and care along with ongoing connection with the wider society? I think there is. Can Culture Care foster models that are challenging enough that participants will develop endurance and resilience and be prepared for generative participation and competition in the wider culture? I know it must.

Cultural Estuaries

Much of the Hudson River, like all the intricate waterways around New York City, is an estuary. In an estuary, salt water mixes with fresh, bringing together multiple ecological layers and habitats to form the world's most diverse and abundant ecosystem.

This abundance arises from an environment that is delicately balanced and often harsh. An environmental scientist recently told me that while an invigorated estuary contains many pockets of homogeneity—like beds of eelgrass or oysters—it is ultimately heterogeneous, for these pockets are all in contact and often in competition with each other. And each pocket is subject to the ebbs and flows of the estuarial system, including variations in salt concentration and sediment from the interaction of river and tidal waters.

Estuaries offer buffer zones for many species. They are a critical nursery area, for example, for young salmon, striped bass, and other fish that come downstream after hatching. Life in semi-protected estuarial wetlands during a critical period of their development readies these fish for life in the ocean.

Oysters are one of the many species that thrive in estuaries. They filter the water for plankton and bacteria to feed themselves, in the process serving a variety of functions critical to the health and the diversity of species in the surrounding ecology. These small creatures are remarkably effective at cleaning the water they inhabit. They even turn some pollutants into pearls in the process. But they can purify some types of pollution only at the cost of polluting themselves. Because of their function as natural filters and the fact that adult oysters do not move, they are an indicator species, "canaries in the coal mines" of their ecosystems.

New York Harbor used to host oyster beds so abundant that New York City in the late 1800s was known as the world's oyster capital. But the famed oyster beds were decimated in the early 1900s by pollution and raw sewage spewing into their habitat. Recently, when the storm surges from Hurricane Sandy in 2012 surprised New Yorkers, the flooding went as far up as 30th Street and destroyed many artworks in the Chelsea arts district. Had the oyster beds been intact, some say that the natural seawall they formed would have mitigated Sandy's damage, so restoring the oyster beds is one of the post-storm responses under consideration.

Estuaries offer a key model for Culture Care. We can think of the river of culture as an estuary, a complex system with a multiplicity of dynamic influences and tributaries. Within it are many nurturing— but not isolated—habitats. Their purpose is not so much *protection as preparation*. Each individual habitat strengthens its participants to interact with the wider environment, making for a diversity that is healthy enough for true competition. Connected habitats allow for exposure to stronger currents, which push participants to build stronger swimming muscles or grow deeper roots, depending on the context, strengthening each for the overall flourishing of the greater cultural ecology.

Understanding cultural communities in this framework reduces the pressure for strict categorization and rigid programming and helps us better serve diverse populations. We might consider some artists and creative catalysts as oysters of the cultural estuary, rooted and making life better around them. Others may be more like salmon, spending only a season in a nurturing habitat before heading out to sea or making their contribution to life upstream. Some of those passing through will return to the estuary, while others may not.

The point is that different callings require different habitats and different types of care; no single agenda or program can serve them all, but all can contribute to the flourishing of the estuary and to the wider environment. In this model, Culture Care happens best in a condition of vigorous diversity and healthy but rigorous competition, responsive to cultural currents. But true diversity moves beyond mere tolerance to respect for the other in the context of our common life. Just as natural estuaries are highly delicate, we also need a macro vision for stewardship that cares for the overall system and respects many types of contributions.

The action of oysters in filtering the water around them—with the byproduct of turning irritants into iridescence—is part of the way a diverse ecosystem can regenerate toward sustainability. But beauty is far more than a byproduct. And culture is far more than sustainable, it is generative by nature. Artists and creative catalysts gathered together may also contribute to larger structures that can serve as a seawall or breakwater against the currents of utilitarianism and commodification that erode our humanity.

There are historical examples of such cultural estuaries. Sixteenth-century Japan, which produced many art forms, including Sen-no-Rikyu, the distinctive vision of tea, became a fantastic cultural estuary as Portuguese and Italian missionaries came into a land of feudal struggles. Early twentieth-century New York City, with exiles coming in from threats abroad and American struggles in the South, created a mixture of influences that birthed Abstract Expressionism and the Harlem Renaissance. Pre-Renaissance Europe, with Ottoman invasions bringing in a mixture of Islamic and Asian cultures into contact with the West, is another example, as are the salons of Paris in the eighteenth and nineteenth centuries.

While this book can only offer a gesture toward identifying and learning from these examples, it will be a worthwhile journey for social scientists and historians to come together to study such past examples for lessons to be applied to Culture Care. Among the questions worth asking: What degree of cultural buffering and exposure is helpful at different stages of personal and communal growth? Can we find ways to keep our "oysters" healthy as they help filter cultural pollution? What connections are helpful between kindred habitats? What critical mass makes for a generative habitat?

Understanding what we do from historical examples from our past, what can we begin to do today? Culture Care begins with generative practice in our everyday lives. We need to create cultural estuaries, each abundant with diversity, and yet providing safe harbor for the creatives journeying through them. Generative practices grow from generative principles. Are our communities open to different expressions of leadership and vision to guide us in the current cultural flux? Are we confident enough in our identities to open the gates to wider cultural pastures? Are we keeping our soil cultivated for growth?

Let's return to our discussion of border-stalkers. Most potential *mearcstapas* start within a community, however close or strained their ties. What might have happened if Emily Dickinson had been affirmed in her idiosyncratic path, had found in life the support that her poems found nearly a century later? What if Vincent van Gogh had found in his church a safe environment to pursue his creativity?

These fanciful questions have no direct answers, as the context of their lives and decisions create a complex matrix of possibilities. Yet their examples are certainly worth pondering as we ask what, practically, a church or community should do when someone like Vincent or Emily—or like C.J.—is in its midst. How do we support artists to act generatively rather than transgressively? Let me sketch out an initial response here. We can deputize them, then form, train, commission, and support them.

First, we can deputize potential *mearcstapas*. We can teach all the members of the community about the role, and then the community can identify potential border-stalkers as they are raised up or welcomed into the community. If we can recognize them earlier in their own development, we can make space for them to grow within and between our normal, comfortable categories and provide consistent care for them as they discern their calling.

Second, we can provide a nurturing environment with a degree of structure or intentionality, in which artists can be trained in the skills necessary for their new roles. This would include a grounding in the "tribal" or group identity, a critical formation. We can provide Soul Care opportunities, spiritual and artistic weight rooms that will militate against isolation and alienation and give them resources for their journeys. We can help them develop and live out their faith identity as noun rather than adjective. We can create places and opportunities for artists to interact with each other inside the community. This might include mentorships, apprenticeships, and regular ongoing opportunities for unstructured connections. All of this will provide context for interactions that will happen concurrently and subsequently outside the community.

Third, we can provide training and practice in exploring the boundaries, interacting with other groups, moving in and out of different identities, finding news of cultural pasturage to be carried back to the community. This might be a more guided exercise in the beginning and a more independent one as they grow. We can be encouraging as they come to value the messy areas of tribal conflict, as they learn new vocabularies and ways of thinking, and begin to report back. We can also affirm these future leaders in developing their skills in generosity and loving the unlovable, helping them call us to remember the poor to whom we are called to bring Good News.

Fourth, the community may want at some point to commission its apprentice or journeyman *mearcstapas* for their next role, moving into the wastelands, the oceans, or wherever they are called.

Finally, the community can provide ongoing support—moral, practical, and financial. For artists who stay nearby their original community, that should go without saying. But those *mearcstapas* who move on should be encouraged to form and maintain connections with other local communities wherever they go, contributing to the life in their new space as well as sending or bringing back news to their commissioning community.

The details of this approach will need to be filled in (I have a few more suggestions in the following chapters), but this model does offer a way to release the full generative efforts of these creatives, who can offer much to our churches and communities and the wider culture. They can cast the appealing vision of beauty in the face of injustice, revealing brokenness and need, modeling love for the unlovable, revealing complexities, brokering reconciliation, teaching us to speak appealingly and persuasively, guiding the whole community through the challenges of engaging with the culture, leading us away from fragmentation and onward toward reintegration, and—perhaps—even uncovering again the Spirit's light in the churches.

Custodians
of Culture Care

In a culture such as ours, bringing home a bouquet of flowers can be a transgressive act. I want here to write of someone who is not an artist, and offer a real-life parable on the Hudson River estuary.

In the early 1960s, Fred Danback came home from the Korean War to work at Anaconda Wire and Cable, a copper wire factory in Hastings-on-Hudson, New York, thirty miles north of Manhattan. It was a booming enterprise. But he soon became troubled by what he saw at the factory. To restore beauty to the river he had grown up with, Danback became a whistleblower against his own company.

In a PBS interview with Bill Moyers, Danback said, "I seen all kinds of oil and sulfuric acid, copper filings; my gosh, they were coming out of that company like it was going out of style ..."[32] He said that shad fishermen started to lose "their business because there was oil in the water that would cause the fish to be contaminated with it, and the Fulton Market refused to take their weekly catch ... [Anaconda] and other businesses were polluting a river and hurting a second business, the shad fishermen. I didn't think they had the right to do that. It used to really infuriate me. I became obsessed with fighting pollution ..."

Fred complained to the managers about his fisherman friends' plight. Each time he did, it seemed, he got demoted. He ended up as a custodian. But Fred never gave up. He worked in that custodian role, literally pushing his broom into every room of the company. He also took copious notes and made maps of the company. What was

---

32 Excerpted from the transcript of *America's First River, Part 2*. PBS/Public Affairs Television, Inc., 2002.

intended as a punishment ended up as the best possible opportunity to spy on the company. He had all the keys!

There were few pollution laws at the time. Fred and a few other pioneers of the environmental movement decided to sue Anaconda under an archaic law called the Refuse Act of 1899, which Fred found while cleaning the local library. In 1972, when the U.S. Attorney's Office found a way to prosecute Anaconda, they used Fred's maps and notes as evidence.

"The company was fined $200,000 under the Refuse Act of 1899, you know ... Even today for a polluter to be fined $200,000 is a big event. Back in the early 1970s, it was a huge event. It was like a thunderclap," said Fred later. Today, three million striped bass go up and down the Hudson because Fred's efforts led to changes in the laws of the land.

I draw three lessons for Culture Care from this story. We need to be willing to sacrifice. We need to remember our first love. We need to be taking copious notes.

First, Culture Care requires sacrifice. We need to be willing to endure demotions, becoming "custodians" of Culture Care. By being demoted for the right reasons, however, we may gain a humble authority, which can work like keys to unlock doors of cultural "factories," giving us opportunities to clean up—and to see what is really going on. Our "keys" are humility, integrity, determination, and hope for things to come. In the current art world in which ego, selfishness, and self-destructiveness abound, we will stand out, eventually, if we have an ounce of human decency and generosity. What if we are willing to serve someone rather than do art for self-expression? What if we collaborated in humility and gave ourselves in service, not expecting the world, or our audience, to agree with us or applaud us?

Second, we need to remember our first love. Bill Moyers asked Fred Danback, "What kept you going?" Danback replied, "I love that river. It's a beautiful river. Look at it. It's your river, its my river; it belongs to everybody. Who's got a right to mess it up? That's the way I feel about it. I still do, to this day." His memory of that beautiful river kept him going through a long struggle.

What keeps us going? Do we keep our first love in focus, or have we become distracted by the need for survival? Your first love as an artist may have been revealed when you drew something on paper that came alive to you. Or perhaps you were playing a character in a school play and you realized you had entered another person's world, a world you never knew existed. Or perhaps as a dancer, you made a single leap that seemed to defy gravity. A first love for creative catalysts may have been when a song began to burn deep within you as a teen, or when you encountered a painting that you had to keep going back to, as something in that work kept opening up new vistas for you.

One way to approach the rediscovery of our first love may be by considering the contrast—what is now causing you to lose hope? Because artists and creative folks are gifted receptors, sensitive to the world's woes, we may be the first to internalize, and be in despair. It is this "first love" that can recognize a world that is "not supposed to be." If we forget it, we will end up being swallowed up in the polluted river and lose our vision for making art—and possibly for living.

Third, we need to take copious notes. Just like Fred Danback, we need to fulfill our responsibilities as custodians of culture—cleaning where we can. We can use our new keys to unlock the workrooms of cultural production. We can take notes to show people the flawed practices that flow out as cultural pollutants, so these can be identified and addressed.

Fred was not an artist, but many readers of this book are. Our notebooks should be filled with drawings, with color and fantastic designs. We are gifted with creativity and expression. Our notes should be beautiful, good, and true.

Stewardship of culture and stewardship of nature go side by side. The activities of the arts are acts of stewardship. Many people see the arts and entertainment as enemies, or at least view them with healthy suspicion, and not without cause. Many recent expressions of the arts have twisted "the good, the true, and the beautiful" in the same way that we have polluted our rivers. The arts are always upstream of culture, and artists are the creators of culture. The question is, how do we enact change?

There's not a day that I do not think of Fred Danback. As I used to jog on the promenade of the river, I thanked God for Fred's sowing the initial seeds of sacrifice. As I follow the bluebirds' nesting behavior at my farmland now, I think of his work to create cleaner rivers and air. But there's more to the story.

As the horrific news began to come out on the airliner attacks of September 11, 2001, the initial estimate of those who perished was twelve to fifteen thousand. In the next few days, however, the numbers kept decreasing, eventually to 2,977—still unbearable, surely. I have a theory about why the initial estimate turned out to be so wrong.

September 11 was the first day of school. There were eight thousand students around the World Trade Center towers. Parents had just dropped off their children—as did my wife with our three—when the sinister shadow of the first plane passed over them in the schoolyard. Few of these parents made it to work. Those who did came back down the steps right away, like many of our friends, ignoring the fatal direction to "stay where you are."

You may not see the connection yet with Fred Danback, but there is a direct link in my mind. Here it is: All of the schools around the towers were built since the late 1970s. Because Danback was willing to be demoted, the river became cleaner. Because the river became cleaner, the parks around the river became attractive. Because the parks were good, young couples becoming parents decided to stay in their small Battery Park apartments instead of escaping to suburbia. Because of the resulting tremendous increase in the student population starting in the late seventies, the city built all those schools.

I am convinced Fred Danback made a difference on 9/11. One person with the courage to be demoted, one person willing to sacrifice for the restoration of beauty, created a ripple effect in culture with immeasurable generative influence. The effects of his action cannot be measured but can only be told in how we live our lives—and so it is worth noting that the children of 9/11, including our three, grew up to be enormously resilient, creative, and community-minded.

Culture Care actions, similarly, cannot be measured by typical metrics of effectiveness and efficiency. The measure of success must be in how our sacrifice to make Culture Care possible manifests itself in the lives of our children.

We need to become a community of Fred Danbacks. We should never forget the beauty of the river of our calling, and we should have the courage to speak and sacrifice on its behalf.

People like Danback awoke us to the beauty of the Hudson River. We no longer see a black river as a good thing or as the inevitable result of "progress." Something shifted in culture on the environmental front, and we need to replicate that shift with culture itself, with the rivers of culture that are now also blackened and uninhabitable with utilitarian pragmatism and over-commodification.

We need not be opposed to industry or capitalism to be Culture Care agents. The problems we face arise not from producing copper wires or being involved in profitable businesses but from a narrowing of our understanding of success to only what is measurable with consumption and utility—and ultimately, from a failure of care and courage.

Business Care

The model of the cultural estuary, a heterogeneous, competitive environment that is preserved toward a thriving culture, applies, in fact, equally to capitalistic ventures, entrepreneurism, and what I have begun to call *Business Care*. Healthy capitalistic competition can also be conducive for the growth of culture. It may be useful to begin this discussion by further defining the term *creative catalysts* as a key ingredient toward Culture Care.

Creative catalysts are those who may not be full time artists, but desire to contribute to creating an enduring shift in the culture of their chosen fields. Catalysts are, by definition, elements that serve generative growth by being present in the mixture of a microcosm. Creative catalysts could be a business CEO, a teacher, a custodian, or even an artist who goes beyond self-expression.

A former board member of International Arts Movement, David Fuller, is a fine example of a creative catalyst. As a bank executive, he felt, at first, out of place attending one of our conferences. But in one of the lectures, he heard another business leader speak of being a "creative catalyst," and helping to "rehumanize" the culture of business around us. He returned from this arts conference and convened a discussion at his Oklahoma City bank. He gathered the banks owners and senior management and led them in asking two questions: 1) How can we as a bank be "rehumanized"? and 2) As a for-profit company, how can we have multiple bottom lines that *care* for our community? Dave recently wrote me an e-mail recounting this journey:

> *We established what we called a Team Fund. It was partially funded by the bank, by individual contributions, and through*

projects like "Jeans Days." Each Friday, employees can wear jeans if they contribute $3 to the Team Fund. The employees at each location decide how money in that fund is used. One day a young mom with two kids in the car came through the drive-thru of one of our small rural locations. Her car died and wouldn't start. Her battery was dead. A couple of our employees pushed her car to the parking lot. Then, with money from their Team Fund, they bought a new battery and installed it for her. It sounds simple but was so profound on many levels.

A creative catalyst modeling and extending rehumanized values created a Culture Care condition. In the ripple effect from one leader, a bank ended up taking care of a single mom in need of help. This single, collaborative act of generosity called for creativity and imagination from both workers and management. This one act has already begun to multiply generatively into the bank's culture, increasing awareness, communication, and loyalty to (and from) customers.

Often business practice and art-making are seen as things at opposing poles on a spectrum of pragmatics and creativity. On one hand, business discipline requires convergent decision-making, narrowing down to a particular focus and a bottom line in a highly organized system. Such a mindset can provide stability to the system, and has been a dominant force in our culture. Artists, on the other hand, are divergent thinkers, often seem to thrive on uncertainty, and are resourceful enough to survive on very little.

Business Care, as an extension of Culture Care, creates a hybrid microcosm, merging the two. In addition, we have learned at IAM that a significant contribution can be made to any growing organization, whether it be business or church, if the "pragmatic" decision-makers *invite* artists to participate in the decision-making process—if analytical thinkers intentionally involve intuitive thinkers. Dave did that by bringing the word "rehumanize" to the context of his bank's decision-making.

I recently had lunch with a business leader. We shared what people were faced with today in our areas of expertise, so I naturally shared a bit about the plight of artists. I then asked him what his clients, who are CEOs and bankers, were facing. He spoke of how bankers, after the Lehman Brothers collapse, now have to justify their work. Many bankers became bankers for stability and high income; they are willing to work hard for that, but they have never had to justify their choice. But now bankers asked "what do you do?" at a party will have to defend and justify continuing in that profession. He said that this is also true of some CEOs.

I am used to defending my decision to be an artist in this pragmatic world. If a banker now has to do the same thing, it occurred to me that a banker and an artist can now have a more meaningful discussion on how they can help each other toward thriving and a vision for a rehumanized culture. In such a conversation, the language of care—for both business and culture—is not only desired, but necessary for all people. We are facing an inflection point in culture that demands more than "bottom line" thinking. We need Business Care.

How a movement begins

I am often asked "How does one create a movement?" In order to start a movement, you need three elements. 1) An artist-type with creative capital, 2) a pastor (or community organizer) type with social capital, and 3) a business type with access to material capital. To illustrate the point when I share this idea with others, I draw a triangle, such as the one below.

Rehumanized Capitalism

Material Capital

What is interesting about this triangle is that if you have two out of the three, you can make what you do sustainable. For instance, if you are creative, and have an abundance of funding, you can continue to create. If you have many friends and are very creative, you will do fine, too. But if you only have one out of three, you are in trouble. Imagine a rich person with no creativity or friends.

Since most of us are not gifted with all three, we will need to partner with those who are different from us. A cultural estuary will likely provide people who are different from us, and we need to begin befriending outside of our area of comfort.

So I encourage someone who wants to begin a Culture Care movement in their region to gather a core group with all three of these types of capital. If you are an artist, find a pastor friend and a business entrepreneur. Two out of three will make what you do sustainable; three out of three can launch a generative movement to which we can invite others.

Practical Advice
for Artists

Many artists struggle to make a living off their work, and I am often asked how I began my career. I begin to answer by speaking of the mindset I have found essential. Being self-supporting is good, but it is also a noble thing to be able to work nine-to-five in an unrelated field—even in a boring job—when this is done purposefully to make art possible. If you are waiting tables, it's one thing to do so to pay your rent, but it is another thing entirely to do so to make your art. In the former mindset, you are in survival mode, barely making it; in the latter, you are always creating, letting your intuition germinate, even as you serve others. This is the generative path.

Many masterpieces of still life paintings from seventeenth and eighteenth century Amsterdam (the Golden Age of Dutch painting) were painted by shopkeepers who sold cheese until early afternoon, then closed up shop and painted for the rest of the day. T. S. Eliot was a banker, Wallace Stevens an insurance salesman, Dana Gioia a marketing executive. These and other notable writers and artists have had day jobs. Some have told me that they create better having a stable work environment. Others even look intentionally for boring bureaucratic work.

Are you called to make art? Make sure to ask this question with a few advisors. It's a good idea, a friend once told my son, to have a "board of directors" for your life. This accountability group should be people you trust—and who can tell you the truth. They can be peers or elder sages, but they should include people with expertise you lack, like lawyers, accountants, or entrepreneurs. You should also include people with experience in the arts who can help you discern your true calling—or its absence.

It is impossible to be an artist today. You must persevere beyond your limits, facing naysayers, your doubts, and your limited abilities. But if painting—or acting, or writing—is the only way you will find your inner thriving, then you must cultivate that art and see if your work can lead to thriving for both yourself and your family. Under such conditions, if you are not deeply convinced of your call, vacillation will cause despair and affect your work.

Raising support

After graduating from college, I knew that I needed to try to make it as an artist. Even though I was not a Christian at the time, I often used the expression "I am called" to describe the inner sense that I had to try to develop my art. I looked for a job that allowed me to paint part time. I was fortunate to find an assistant teaching position in a local special education school. The story of Judy bringing home a bouquet of flowers came at that time. Even my failure to be an artist then turned out, in the long run, to be a generative experience.

Later on, when I discovered that it was Christ who was calling me, it occurred to me that he would also care about me enough to supply my needs and those of my family. Christ reveals an infinite God and he commands us to "seek God's Kingdom and God's righteousness first, and all these things will be added unto you" (Matthew 6). I have come to recognize that God does not promise an easy path, but an abundant path.

I found myself in a community of missionaries who helped me to understand my new journey as a Christian. I became convinced that God had called me back into the arts after my "transfer of allegiance" to Christ. I was sure of my calling and my missionary friends seemed sure of theirs. So I asked, "how do you make your calling sustainable?" They told me that they raised support. They went around to all their friends and contacts, as well as many churches, and let them know of their call to be missionaries in Japan. In the process, they sharpened their articulation of their calling and tested that sense of calling.

I was a graduate student, with a wife and a child now. I thought, "Well, I am called to be an artist, so how do we apply this to my art?" I had a few successful shows—which means a few pieces sold and I had a good review in the Japan Times—and a few people became interested in my work and would come visit me in my studio. I began to ask if they would be willing to support me as an artist for a year. I asked them not to pay me up front to purchase a piece, but to pay me in monthly installments. I figured this would help me to learn to budget, and it turned out so. Soon I had six or seven people willing to do this, paying, for example, $100 a month and coming to the studio at the end of the year to pick a work worth $1,200. Combined with my scholarship, I was able to sustain a living with my art, even as a graduate student.

I then went to a gallery interested in my work and told them that I wanted to do a show, but that half of the works in the exhibit would already have been sold due to this arrangement. I told the gallery that having half of the paintings sold, with red dots next to them, as the show opened, would give the exhibit momentum. They agreed. This is how I got my start. It came out of my need to support my family, but even today, what I do is based on the same model.

Most of the "collectors" who first purchased my works were Japanese "salary men." They were not wealthy but they loved art. Many of them supported me for the duration of my stay in Japan and then donated the works they bought to museums. I was very fortunate. None of the collectors in the first ten years of my career were "Christian" collectors.

Three G's for artists

More recently, in moving toward Culture Care, I have come to also realize that it's beneficial to think and pray not just towards sustainability, but generativity. Let's apply the "three G's" at an individual level.

1) *Genesis moments*—Every moment can be a genesis moment, and artists are often attuned to this reality more than most. A visit by a

collector to a studio can be an opportunity to serve the collector and create such moments. A generatively focused collector will likely be more interested in learning from the creative process and helping the artist toward thriving.

Of course, the art market includes galleries and even collectors who treat art as strict transaction. I try to avoid both (which means I am limiting my career quite a bit). I consider it a privilege when people visit my studio or an exhibit to purchase a painting. My prayer is that my art will continue to create genesis moments in their lives.

It may also help to consider the potential for genesis moments as a point of perspective when speaking with potential purchasers. People balk at buying art that is, let's say, $1,200. It seems like a lot of money, and it is a sacrifice to most people. It is also only $100 a month—approaching the price of a movie outing for a family of five. A movie seen with your family is memorable, but ephemeral. An artwork you own can provide years of genesis moments in your own home, and you are investing in generativity as well by helping an artist continue her work.

2) *Generosity*—I've found that artists can be the most generous people in the world. When we hold auctions or other fund requests for IAM, it is always the artists who send in their works (framed and ready for hanging), show up to volunteer, and even send checks. One time we received a check for $5 from an artist. I knew that this was a great sacrifice for her, and I had tears in my eyes as I thanked her. She said she was ashamed by the amount, but I assured her that her gesture meant more to the staff than she realized. Artists need to lead in generosity in society and in the church, for they are in regular touch with the gratuity of the created order. God created gratuitously, and so can we.

3) *Generational*—The arts are generative by nature, so people regardless of their faith dispositions find themselves thinking generationally. At any good museum you will see works from five hundred years ago. Fra Angelicos and Michaelangelos, da Vincis and Raphaels. Have you ever thought that somehow, what you do or

make can last five hundred years? It is possible but unlikely that our works will be known that long from now. But a faithful community to steward culture will mean the creation of many works of art that will inspire future generations to create toward that five-hundred-year vision. What you make now may be done to prepare the foundation for your children and subsequent generations to find thriving. This may cost status or success, but some art could be a sacrificial offering toward future thriving.

If you are a supporter of the arts, try fitting what you do into this five-hundred-year quest as well. Your small investment today to help an artist, a dancer, or a theatre group, could be a stone thrown into the pond of culture, its ripple effect more substantial than your own immediate experience.

Ten years later, at an artist talk at my gallery, I complained about the fact that most of the collectors who purchased the works I have made in response to God's call were non-Christians. I said that since I was creating art as a calling, I wanted some of my works to go to Christians' homes. A Philadelphia pastor was in the audience. He became the first pastor to purchase one of my prints. I knew that he was sacrificing to commit to this, and something of a weight fell from my shoulders as I heard it. I felt affirmed in my calling. That pastor is now president of a major Christian college. Every time I think of my calling, I think of his act and how much his single purchase encouraged me.

Attitude matters. Even if you are truly called, you will find occasions to complain when circumstances do not align with that sense of call. This is different from an attitude of entitlement that is enraged when the world does not instantly support you (I avoid the work of young artists with such an view). But a "complaint" coming out of your calling is more invitation than demand. As I spoke of a lack of Christian collectors in my life, I was smiling, and I remember it being less a demand than a prayer.

Having a positive outlook in adversity should be one of the main factors you consider in recognizing your calling. Rather than giving up because of the many, many closed doors we face as artists, and rather than being angry at the world for "our art not meeting the needs of the world," we can rejoice in our lack, as it is ultimately God, the grand Artist, who will answer our call, and provide bread for our journey.

"Blessed are those who are persecuted for righteousness sake," says Jesus in Matthew 5:10. He is speaking to artists as much as any other group of his followers. An artist is called by God just as much as any missionary or church. All of us, artists and others alike, will face some degree of struggle in responding to our call. But we are all called into love, and we need to be bold in declaring our calls. For artists who create through such a calling toward a greater Love, art is at the core of their reality, their very existence. Just as Emily Dickinson had to write, as Vincent Van Gogh had to paint, as Mahalia Jackson had to sing, so must we journey on to create a greater condition of awareness, a new vista of care for all.

New Vocabularies, New Stories

The overall strategy of Culture Care is to create cultural estuaries. Our reading groups, churches, and schools can become microcosms of care. All can participate in the process. As we are seeing, before we can begin to create such harbors, we will have to reexamine some conventionally held cultural viewpoints, and inject new vocabulary into our cultural dialogues, moving away from culture wars to Culture Care. Let me end with an example.

On a visit to Biola University, I spoke with a photographer who had graduated from its art department. She creates works of art and also uses her craft as a wedding photographer to make a living. As we discussed Culture Care, we agreed that the phrase "taking a photograph" is problematic. When we "take" a photograph, what exactly are we doing? Are we taking that person's image as some in the movie *Lawrence of Arabia* thought of photographs—like stealing a person's soul?

The paparazzi's "taking" of celebrity photos for commercial gain, or for the sheer excitement of exposing a scandalous moment, seems indeed to take away someone's soul, treating the subject as somehow more thing than human. Might not this contribute to the way many celebrity actors and musicians seem to get caught in a drained and zombie-like existence, desensitized, and alienated from their own natural gifts that should be conveying to others a deep, embedded sense of humanity. Photographic taking also accentuates a culture-wars mindset, manipulating images to amplify the divide.

This photographer and I arrived together at a fine alternative. What if we "gifted" photographs instead of "taking" them? Might it be possible to practice photography as a gift to the person at whom one points the camera? How might a commercial photographer modify the transactional nature of that work to make a living, and even better, be generative? This may seem to be a simple, and even innocent, approach. But words are powerful. The mindset going into a shoot and how we speak about photographs can be, just like Scout in *To Kill a Mockingbird*, a way both prophetic and innocent at the same time.

We are attempting to contribute to this type of reimagining at International Arts Movement. IAM is also a place of experimentation to see if such a movement of changed perceptions can be implemented in a photographer's studio, at an artist's easel, from a theater stage. So as we journey forward, I urge you to journey with us. If anything in this book has stirred your heart, please begin to apply the principles in your lives and your art, and let us know what happens.

Remember: our failure to think and act generatively, and our awareness of that failure, is the first step toward generativity. A Culture Care gathering may simply, at first, look like a group of people admitting that we fail to be generative, but are willing to ask for input from each other. Becoming generative is a constant principle and a continuing process. We need to acknowledge that we, in ourselves, may not have the power to regenerate what is "decomposing" in front of us or to push back against a culture that is dying. But, by making this the starting point, we may tap into what Wendell Berry called "the gift of the land," the gift of culture.

May our work be seeds into the soil of culture. Better yet, may these conversations strengthen our hands to cultivate that soil, so that the good seed can take root deeply and flourish. May our cultural garden, our cultural orchard, become a place of shelter for many creatures, including our own grandchildren. May we stalk the borders and margins, accepting our deputized call to carry Good News to the poor.

Let me finally answer the question I raised in the beginning of this introduction to Culture Care, "Do we *need* beauty in our lives?" If we desire to be fully human, the answer is yes, absolutely.

But we can now see that even this question, following the flow of thoughts so far, is ultimately utilitarian. We must shift from asking "what we need" to "what we long for."

The biblical vision for flourishing of our lives, lived fully under God's love, includes the beautiful. This is what we long for. What about you? What do you long for? Can beauty point to that reality? How you live out the answer to these questions is up to you. But the pursuit of these questions will lead to the feeding of our souls.

What If?

What if each of us endeavored to bring beauty into someone's life today in some small way?

What if we, by faith, saw each moment as a genesis moment, and even saw the current problems we are facing as genesis opportunities?

What if, instead of treating the independence and creativity of artists as problems to solve, we found in them opportunities for a new type of leadership in our current cultural flux?

What if artists became known for their generosity rather than only their self-expression?

What if art school became a place to train Culture Care agents, rather than a filter that only lets through artists who can "make it"?

What if we considered our actions, decisions, and creative products in light of five hundred years and multiple generations?

What if we started to transgress by integrating our faith, art, and life—and speaking boldly about them?

What if we committed to speaking fresh creativity and vision into culture rather than denouncing and boycotting other cultural products?

What if we saw art as gift, and not just as commodity?

What if we empower the "border-stalkers" in our communities, support and send them out?

What if we, like Mahalia Jackson, stood behind our preachers, or our MLK, Jr.'s, and exhorted them to "tell 'em about the Dream!"

What if we created songs to draw people into movements for justice and flourishing?

What if we made things in secret, like Emily Dickinson, knowing that the world may not yet be ready for our thoughts?

What if we became custodians of culture, willing to be demoted for standing up for what is right, but taking copious notes so we can challenge the status quo?

What if we assumed that relational and creative capital is infinite? What kind of effect would that have on our business practices?

What if we "gifted" photographs to share the light of the miraculous in people, rather than "take" photographs so that we can own them and sell them?

Note down your own "what if?" statements, and share them with friends. Consider ways you can help these statements birth a plan for your community.

Your "what ifs?"

_____

_____

_____

_____

_____

_____

_____

_____

_____

_____

_____

_____

_____

_____

_____

A Gratuitous
Postscript

Golden Sea was the result of a gratuitous act of creativity. While working intensely and semi-sequestered on the year-and-a-half project of *The Four Holy Gospels*, I needed a reprieve from the detail work of 140 pages of small illuminations. So I took a large canvas, stretched Kumohada paper over it, and began to work on it, without any purpose for the piece. No exhibit awaited it, and I had not even a theme for it. It was a playground for my intuition, a gift to allow for materials to be layered and my soul to be nurtured, so that when I sat to work on the illuminations, I could draw on that freedom of movement and expression.

The resulting painting, now called *Golden Sea*, has become one of the seminal works of my career. My son Ty was hired by Crossway, publisher of *The Four Holy Gospels*, to take videos for that project. When he came into the studio while I was working on the illuminations, he asked me, "Hey, what's that painting?" It then included over sixty layers of minerals and applied gold. "I don't know," I said. "It's something I've been working on." He paused to look. "It has everything you've ever done in it."

About two weeks later, Valerie Dillon, owner of Dillon Gallery in New York, which represents my works, came in to see the illuminations and made a similar observation. As we discussed our upcoming retrospective catalogue, she said, "of course, that painting will be on the cover, right?"

Sometimes, the best work comes out in the daily discipline of working, when you are least expecting it. It is gratuitous, and at first peripheral, but then it reveals the core of who you are, as your intuition knows what needs to be expressed even before your rational mind, or the market, does.

I advise young artists always to do some work in secret, whether it be paintings that you never intend to show, or a poem that you do not have to send to a publisher. Art resists being limited to utilitarian "career making." Our intuition seems to crave the fully human abundance of joy, which is connected to God's act of gratuitous creation. God does not need us to exist; we do not fulfill God's needs. We are created in love, and the cosmos abounds with the delight of the Creator who created for love and wonder—and gives us a role to play in extending both.

Start now, today, to place that secret work in your "Emily Dickinson desk." May your intuition be nourished by the gift you have been given.

May our lives, our faith, and our art reflect and extend that gratuitous love and wonder.

May we always be willing to present a bouquet of flowers, even to an artist—or a culture—who may not yet know that they desire beauty.